KU-732-232

KEY TO MAP (*by ethnic "nation" areas*)

TLINGIT
1. Yakutat
2. Skagway
3. Haines and Port Chilkoot
4. Klukwan and Chilkat
5. Juneau, capital of Alaska
6. Sitka
7. Wrangell
8. Klawock
9. Ketchikan and Saxman
10. Cape Fox and Tongas
    (by 1900 the Kaigani-Haida of Prince of Wales Island claimed these old townsites)

HAIDA
11. Tuxecan
12. Kasaan
13. Howkan and Long Island
14. Yan
15. Massett
16. Skidegate
17. Tsal
18. Skedans, Tanu, Tasu
19. Ninstints (on Anthony Island)

TSIMSYAN
20. Prince Rupert
21. Gitrhahla
22. Port Simpson
23. Fort Simpson
24. Kitwancool
25. Kitwanga
26. Hazelton and Kispiox
27. Kitsemkaelem
28. Kitimat
29. Hartley

BELLA COOLA
30. Bella Coola and Talio

KWAKIUTL
31. Princess Royal Island
32. Bellabella
33. Blunden Harbour
34. Fort Rupert
35. Koskimo
36. Alert Bay
37. Kelsey Bay

NOOTKA
38. Quatsino
39. Kyuquot
40. Nootka Sound and Nootka
41. Clayoquot Sound
42. Barkeley Sound, Sproat Lake, Alberni
43. Nitinat and Clo-oose
44. Cape Flattery, Makah, Neah Bay

COAST SALISH
45. Campbell River
46. Powell River
47. Squamish
48. Harrison Hot Springs and Chilliwack
49. Vancouver
50. Port Alberni
51. Nanaimo
52. Cowichan Lake and Duncan
53. Victoria (Songhees), capital of British Columbia
54. Bellingham
55. Tullalip and Everett
56. Seattle
57. Tacoma and Puyallup
58. Chimaukum, Sequim, Port Townsend
59. Port Angeles
60. Forks
61. Lake Quinault and Amanda Park
62. Queets
63. Hoquiam and Aberdeen
64. Olympia, capital of Washington

QUILLIUTE
65. La Push and Hoh

HIGHWAYS

Canadian No. 12 and No. 97 link Vancouver with the Alaska Highway, which begins at Dawson Creek. Canadian No. 16 extends southwest from Hazelton, via the Skeena River valley, to Prince Rupert on the coast. The major Southeast Alaska highway links Tlingit land, at Haines-Port Chilkoot, with the Yukon portion of the Alaska Highway.

THE
TOTEM
POLE
INDIANS

THE TOTEM POLE INDIANS

Joseph H. Wherry

ILLUSTRATED

Wilfred Funk, Inc.
NEW YORK

Copyright © 1964 by Joseph H. Wherry
Library of Congress Catalogue Card Number 64–20968
Design: Betty Crumley

Special sketches by L. D. Sutton.
Unless otherwise credited, photographs by the author

Jacket photo: A Kwakiutl house front and
memorial pole in Thunderbird Park, Victoria,
British Columbia.

To my wife's mother who, unlike Gunah-kah-daht's wife's mother,
is a wonderful mother-in-law.

Contents

THE
TOTEM
POLE
INDIANS

Preface

We drove the Indians out of the land,
But a dire revenge these redmen planned,
For they fastened a name to every nook,
And every boy with a spelling book
Will have to toil till his hair turns gray
Before he can spell them the proper way.

On the Cape,
—Eva March Tappan

Kla-ha-ya!

The least known of all the aboriginal peoples of North America are the Indians of the Pacific Northwest Coast. As unique in their culture as they were isolated, their descendants have, nevertheless, suffered the loss of virtually everything including dignity in a hundred years of legislation as damaging to their customs as to the accurate telling of their history in most accounts in the popular press.

Born and raised in the southern area of "Totemland," the author's first recollection of the name applied to these Indians was "Siwash." This appellation, as sometimes used, is as insulting as it is inaccurate. Highly skilled in a variety of arts and crafts, the Northwest Coast natives could scarcely be called "savage" were one to study their regional culture. Yet it is from the French word *sauvage*, inserted crudely into the Chinook jargon, that "Siwash" has crept into the Northwest idiom of old-timers and newcomers alike.

The regional native arts and mythology have been distorted in meaning even more. In this decade a large West Coast newspaper gave full-color prominence to a tapestry with the caption: "Ancient deity is subject of tapestry from Mexico." The symbol portrayed was a stylized grizzly bear, not native to Mexico but exactly duplicating a well-known Tlingit house-front painting in Alaska.

The most famous and impressive products of an aboriginal way of life, superior and unique when compared to native cultures elsewhere in the New World, have been similarly dishonored. Totem poles, the trademark of the Pacific Northwest, have been popularly ascribed to Indians generally, and to those as far removed as the Seminole, the woodland Sioux before their forced westward migration, and even the tribes of the arid Southwest.

Bigots, who refused to investigate the purposes (note the plural) of these carvings of all sizes and shapes, early came to the erroneous conclusion that they were mysterious idols to be worshiped. Others, with the trappings of government authority—principally in coastal British Columbia—prevented the continuation of the supreme native ceremony. In the latter case, the "potlatch"—the Indian name for the totem-pole-raising ceremony—had admittedly got somewhat out of hand around Prince Rupert and was threatening to impoverish many Indians.

From the Indian standpoint, however, the pressure of European culture had compressed the Indians into a social and economic situation that left them no alternative but to carry their gift-giving to an extreme in a final effort to maintain their social and cultural traditions.

If the author appears, in the following chapters, to be an "Indian lover," then so be it. With pleasant memories of childhood days spent fishing with an aged Indian chief still fresh in mind, the author confesses to the belief that there is much to learn from the wisdom and even from the mythology of these ancient peoples. When an old Indian—a Squamish as nearly as can be remembered—gave a toy dugout canoe, carved in the image of the great ones his fathers used in navigating Puget Sound, to a seven-year-old boy, it sparked a determination to write a tribute to these Indians someday.

This book is partly the result of such recollections. Seeing a pitiful few canoes sailing toward the setting sun in the mid-twenties brought from the author's father the explanation that "the Indians are going to a potlatch." I hope they arrived safely, for I know they were going *not* to worship pagan gods carved on cedar poles, but rather to honor a descendant of a once-noble clan or tribe. In honor to the past they would hear of the deeds of ancestors and be reminded that "in the beginning" a Power higher than themselves created them and had revealed a knowledge—now misty with time—of the greatness of the universe.

Though our annual calendar is full, there is one special day lacking: an American Indian Day. We took their lands and stifled their culture. It is high time we recognized a great tradition of which this book can cover only a small part.

J.H.W.

1

Totemland—
Its People and Their Origin

The encouraging increase of interest in our country's heritage has generally by-passed the most colorful area between the two seas, and particularly the amazing cultural attainments of the Northwest Pacific Coast Indians.

When Europeans arrived, the Indians of this region were living a more bountiful life than any other Amerinds of the discovery era. By the time European culture had fully embraced them, their numbers had been tragically decreased from an estimated sixty thousand to less than half that number by the white man's firewater, his penchant for centralized authority, and most of all by his diseases. There was less warfare between whites and the Indians of Totemland than elsewhere principally because these Indians had nowhere to go: the Pacific Ocean prevented any retreat.

The region—which I like to call Totemland—sprawls northwestward from Grays Harbor in Washington to the Malaspina Glacier in southeast Alaska, about 200 miles, as the raven flies, northwest of Juneau. This narrow strip west of the Cascade Mountains comprises the Olympic Peninsula, the area immediately around Puget Sound, southwestern British Columbia including Vancouver Island, and the Alaskan panhandle. Heavily timbered, and roughly 1,050 miles long, Totemland is rarely as much as 100 miles wide on the mainland.

Totemland Indians' height averages nearly 5 feet, 9 inches in the north, with many as tall as 6 feet among the Tlingit. The height of the Haida and Tsimsyan is only slightly less. Stature decreases proportionately toward the south: the Salish tribes of coastal British Columbia average only about 5 feet, 3 inches, but the Olympic Peninsula Salish are slightly taller. The Nootka including their Makah tribesmen around Cape Flattery, Washing-

La Push town is the seat of the little Quilliute nation. The fine, though small, harbor shelters fishing and pleasure craft. Just south of Cape Flattery, Washington, this is typical coastal Totemland terrain.

ton's northwesternmost tip, are between the above two extremes in average height, as are the Kwakiutl and Bella Coola.

Their most outstanding physiological characteristic—and this took the early European explorers by surprise—is the profusion of facial hair among the males. Mustaches and beards were commonly noted in the earliest records, in marked contrast to Indians everywhere outside this geographical region. The frequently wavy hair emphasizes the physical contrast with Indians elsewhere. Rather than the jet-black color popularly believed to be universal among Indians, a very dark brown prevails. The skin color varies from as light as southern Europeans, in the northern nations, to a somewhat darker hue toward the Puget Sound area. Nowhere in Totemland, however, does the skin coloring of the natives conform to the "redskin" concept so ingrained into American folklore.

As a matter of fact, the first European to explore the Bella Coola country, famed Alexander Mackenzie, whose name is legend in Canada, discovered that these ethnic relatives of the Coast Salish and Kwakiutl often had hair of a rich brown shade and comparatively light-colored eyes. Investigating anthropologists and enthnologists, during the past century, disclosed no definitely established reasons for this provocative variation.

A muscular race of fairly stocky build, these Indians all have rather wide faces and large heads, especially the northernmost ones. The latter are also very long-limbed with proportionately shorter bodies while these physical features are reversed toward the southern nations. Shoulders and chests everywhere tend to be quite broad with pronounced upper torso development. From this, one may logically assume that the regional commitment to the maritime life—with consequent greater use of arm and shoulder muscles—was responsible for the physical development from that time in prehistory when their forebears burst into North America.

This brings us to the racial origin of these ingenious Indians. Physical appearances alone suggest that of all the migrations science justifiably believes to have originated in Asia, that of the Totemland Indians is the most recent because these peoples resemble Asiatics more than do other Amerinds. Furthermore—and contrary to a fairly popular misconception—these Indians are *not* "southern" Eskimos. The latter, considerably darker, are ethnically quite different, although the northernmost Tlingit did once share some cultural relations through trade and geographical conflict with southern Eskimo tribes.

To be more specific, the Indians of Totemland bear close physical resemblance to some Mongol and Siberian tribes. Despite extensive expeditions and sundry anthropological investigations during the past several score years, there is still no concrete evidence to prove unquestionably such a northeast Asiatic origin. Within historic times—now approaching five hundred years with regard to North America—the cultures of the two areas under question bear only the most superficial resemblance. Thus, the evidence is that if migrations did occur across what we now call the Bering Sea, the time was very remote, perhaps as much as eight or ten thousand years ago or more. In support of this latter possibility are artifacts found in the Northwest made of organic materials that, under carbon-14 testing, turn out to be upward of eight thousand years old.

In the author's opinion the most sensible conclusion is that there were, during the misty ages of antiquity, many migrations. Quite possibly, as Thor Heyerdahl has pointed out, there have even been countermigrations from North America to Polynesia. Thus, movements about the Pacific Ocean, in both hemispheres, may well add up—if proof is ever discovered—to a veritable migratory cycle. Air and sea creatures engage in such enterprise—why not human beings?

Such considerations are not, as some might suppose, at all far afield. One does, however, run smack up against the modern Bishop Ushers, who will say that such theorizing is sheer lunacy in the light of Biblical revelation, which places man's earthly origin as approximately six thousand years ago. In countering such a claim, however, it is relevant to examine the first two verses of Genesis, Chapter 1. The original *creation*, told of therein, included "the heaven and the earth" in verse 1. Then we find in verse 2 that "void" and "darkness" prevailed. Many theologians, of the related Christian and Jewish faiths, believe that untold ages of time came and went between these two verses.

Why is this worthy of consideration in relation to the origins of our Northwest Coast Indians? Simply because, as already mentioned, items of archaeological interest, exceeding in

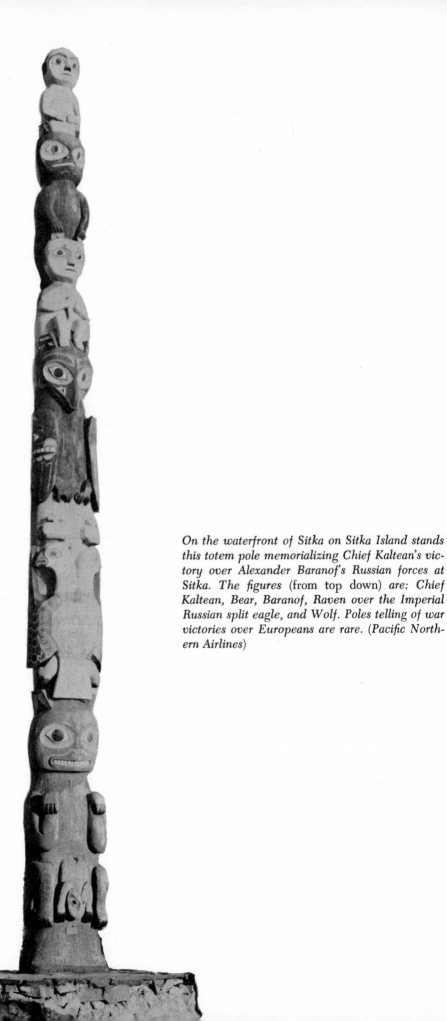

On the waterfront of Sitka on Sitka Island stands this totem pole memorializing Chief Kaltean's victory over Alexander Baranof's Russian forces at Sitka. The figures (from top down) are: Chief Kaltean, Bear, Baranof, Raven over the Imperial Russian split eagle, and Wolf. Poles telling of war victories over Europeans are rare. (Pacific Northern Airlines)

The Coast Salish tribes in Washington carved fewer poles than the northern nations. Often their carvers made quite realistic human likenesses. This preserved figure is in the Quinault tribal country near Lake Quinault.

LEFT: *Depending upon the tribe and clan of the owner, this duplicate of a conventionalized totem crest symbol could be either of supernatural Eagle or of Thunderbird. The vertical design behind the eye denotes a bird tail while the symbol above the mouth generally indicates either inner spirit or symbolizes a joint, in the stylization of the Northwest Coast totem carvers.* RIGHT: *Supernatural Raven, said to have released the sun from the Creator's box (at his feet) "in the beginning," is a tradition almost certainly originating in Siberia, where the Kamchadal called him Kutqua. To the Chuckchee he was Valvivak and subordinate to the Creator, and on the Koryak coast he was called Big Grandfather. This famous old Tlingit post now stands preserved in the park in Saxman, Alaska. (Pacific Northern Airlines)*

age the recognized four thousand years B.C. of Genesis 1:2, have been found on this continent. Bible students need not quake: the author is *not* about to attempt to destroy anyone's faith, including his own. I ask only that we read Genesis 1:28 with perception instead of the customary haste with which this verse is usually treated. What do we discover with regard to what may well be a comparatively recent revelation of just one aspect of creation? The Creator, in the Garden, told "male and female" to "replenish the earth." This seems to verify clearly the existence of a previous race of men prior to whatever catastrophe occurred that brought "darkness" to the earth. Otherwise, the Creator would *not* have said "replenish." One does not replenish something previously nonexisting.

The Indians of Totemland have their own versions of how "there was light." It may be quite presumptuous on our part to label *all* parts of such accounts myth. Later we shall look at their most prominent and regionally universal creation story that places their Eden at the mouth of the Nass River.

It is an established historical fact that racial movements have radiated outward from the ancient cradle of civilization. Moreover the evidence, including physical appearances and productive capabilities, unwaveringly suggests an Asiatic origin. We need not rely on theory alone. It is likely that early-Christian-era Chinese Buddhist monks visited the Northwest Pacific Coast. Just as likely, science agrees, is that ancestors of these Indians did come "out of the foam" as their own tradition relates. This could have happened at any time in prehistory and probably did more than once. The antiquity of the regional belief in Thunderbird reinforces such thinking. That great supernatural spirit bird is said to be of Siberian origin as are the Bear Mother tradition and others.

Having thus considered the most significant reasons for accepting the Asiatic origin of the aborigines of Totemland, our fascination is increased by the following northern historic tradition. Note how neatly this ancient story—how old no one knows—fits in with what science has assumed after years of intense investigation.

From "out of the foam" they came, according to the best-known migration tradition of the Tsimsyan, Haida, and Tlingit. This was the migration of the clan of Salmon-Eater, or Gitrhawn, which later evolved into the Eagle clans of these three northern nations:

Chief Gitrhawn was leading the canoes of his clan on a long journey occasioned by the great deluge that figures so prominently in Northwest Coast lore. The canoes of the fleet became separated in the wildly foaming waters so, with only *six* loaded canoes remaining, Gitrhawn landed after many days on a strange shore inhabited by people speaking an unknown tongue. According to this migration story, said to be true (an *adaorh*), the people of this land were Rhaida, the Haida in the Tsimsyan language, belonging to the Grizzly Bear clan. The newcomers were well received and established a village of their own opposite the Rhaida town.

Now Gitrhawn's most precious possession was a cormorant-skin cap that he wore as a symbol of rank whenever the weather turned bad. According to tradition—and scientific investigations corroborate this—Gitrhawn's new village was somewhere in the northern part of the Queen Charlotte Islands, a hundred or so miles southwest of modern Ketchikan. Food proved plentiful, the Rhaida inhabitants hospitable, and the wayfarers readily learned the island language.

Romance soon blossomed between the nephew of Chief Ka'it, the Haida chief of the Grizzly Bear clan, and Chief Gitrhawn's niece Dzalarhons. According to Rhaida custom, the uncles of the prospective bride and groom conducted the formal arrangements. (The society was matriarchal, the most common Totemland organization.) The nephew's uncles, therefore, carried the bride, dressed in her ceremonial finery, from her uncle's house to the shore and placed her regally on moose-skin-covered boards between two dugouts that were lashed together. The royal wedding party then proceeded across a bay to Chief

Ka'it's Haida village, where the bridegroom waited.

Dzalarhons' clothing befitted a young chieftainess: two fine sea-otter-skin robes and an outer cloak or robe of leather trimmed with dentalia (*tseek*). The latter shells could indicate that the Gitrhawn clan was by this time well established because the northern tribes obtained this valued shell by trading with Vancouver Island tribes two hundred or more miles to the southeast. Tradition explains that dresses or skirts were unknown "in the old days," so the princess wore leather trousers as was customary in ancient times on both sides of the North Pacific Ocean.

After the wedding and festivities, the bride and bridegroom went to their house where the bridegroom lay down to sleep. Dzalarhons did not rest, however, but complied with her husband's bidding that she hold a lighted pitchwood torch over her husband as he slept. When the torch burned short, she protected her arm with her fine leather robe that by sunrise was badly burned. The uncle of the bridegroom rebuked him for such rudeness to his bride and warned that this would surely cause trouble. Chief Ka'it knew Gitrhawn's clan would not look lightly on such treatment of their chief's niece.

The bridegroom, though, did not mend his selfish ways and, after several such nights, all of Dzalarhons' fine sea-otter skins and leather garments were ruined. When her nakedness, due to the bridegroom's tyranny, was discovered, one of the Grizzly Bear clan elders offered her a Haida bearskin robe. This she refused. Stepping outside unclothed, she met her own uncles who were bringing food and gifts to the bridegroom according to Salmon-Eater custom. When Dzalarhons related the recent events, her uncles hastened to Chief Gitrhawn.

Soon the warriors of Dzalarhons' clan descended upon Ka'it's village with her uncle, Gitrhawn, leading them. When his warriors could not find the princess, they attacked the Grizzly Bear clan village. The fighting was severe, with many of each side falling. The Gitrhawn forces prevailed and then began to search for their lost princess. After some time they discovered a statue in stone of a young woman whose legs straddled a creek that seemed to be flowing from her. Chief Gitrhawn knew this statue was his lost niece, Dzalarhons, who had been so shamefully treated by her new husband.

The legend's length prevents a complete telling here, but it contains many incidents that have a relationship to northeast Asiatic folklore. Gitrhawn's own son, with the impetuosity of youth, insisted on wearing the cormorant-skin hat of his father—the chief—on a fishing trip to the lake formed by the rivulet flowing from Dzalarhons' stone statue; because hereditary power descended through the female side of families, this was very wrong. One after another the men led by the chief's son fell dead after being pursued by the fiery figure of a woman carrying a staff surmounted by a large copper-colored frog. When the frog was killed, a volcano erupted and engulfed the Rhaida village.

After a series of disasters and escapes, a lone Gitrhawn woman married a Gitrhahla (Tsimsyan) chief, whose people—in *six* canoes—had rescued her. This young Gitrhawn (or Salmon-Eater clan descendant) woman had somehow managed, during the volcanic eruption, to obtain her chief's cormorant-skin cap.

When she bore her first son to the Gitrhahla chief, she named him Gitrhawn, and in this way the name came to the Gitrhahla people in the Nass River country. This son became a great chief whose descendants went far up the Skeena River into what is now Gitksan-Tsimsyan country. Other descendants, Gitrhawns, migrated north into the Tlingit country and so were spread the traditions and name of Salmon-Eater, whose clan came "over the foam" after the flood into southeast Alaska in ancient times.

As this family grew, the mother one day told her sons to go back to the clan's first home in Haida country and take their grandfather a gift of food. Two sons and a daughter started for the Queen Charlotte Islands in a canoe. Seeing an attractive beach, against the forewarnings of their mother they stopped to rest. A sudden storm damaged their canoe and destroyed much of the food.

For several days they were marooned. Then a strange man appeared, who they realized was a supernatural being. Hearing their tale of woe, the being changed into a great bird and took the young Gitrhahla Gitrhawns under his wings. In his mouth he put two stones; then he flew high over the water.

Halfway across to Haida land the great spirit bird dropped a stone that became a large rock in the straits, which can be seen to this day. He dropped another on an island beach near a Gitrhahla village where it, too, can still be seen if you know where to look! Finally landing the three young people in Haida land, the being warned them not to look up until he had disappeared. The beat of his wings made a great roar and, unable to restrain her curiosity, the young woman peeked and discovered their benefactor was the giant supernatural Eagle-of-the-Sea.

Knowing he had been seen, the monster Eagle dived into the sea and appeared to sink. After this, the Gitrhahla clan people of the Tsimsyan carved stone eagles and took the great supernatural Eagle as their clan crest. With the increase of the family that began with the one remaining Gitrhawn princess, the Salmon-Eater tradition spread throughout the three northern nations as did the Eagle clan

Once standing at Kitimat, about fifty miles up the Douglas Channel in British Columbia, was this old thirty-feet-tall totem pole showing the legendary Dzalarhons wearing the traditional tall hat with four cylindrical sections. Below Dzalarhons are Halibut and Frog, both with heads down. The significance of the last two figures being head down is not known; this could have been in ridicule or for some other now-forgotten tribal reason. Frog played an important part in the Salmon-Eater tradition while Halibut, an important guardian spirit, is rarely seen on totem poles.

crest and story of the cormorant-skin cap. The great Eagle-of-the-Sea had a white head. Consequently, on many northern totem poles, the Eagle at the top is bald or appears to be. He was usually carved with a downward curving beak very much like Thunderbird's. Of course the two great birds are somewhat related in the many confusing myths of Totemland. Far up the Skeena River another monster bird, Giant Woodpecker, has similar attributes. Southward, among the Nootka, Sea Gull performed similar supernatural chores.

A number of years ago an anthropologist, Marius Barbeau of the National Museum of Canada, interpreted the Salmon-Eater tradition as a factually based story of a migration eastward along the Aleutian Islands and reckoned this journey probably began somewhere on the Siberian coast. Early in this century, Dr. J. R. Swanton of the Smithsonian Institution recorded versions of the same tradition. Both of these eminent authorities found living elders of a Tsimsyan Eagle clan of the Gitrhahla tribe around the mouth of the Nass River. Each is also inclined to believe this tradition is relatively recent, but neither explains the story's reference to the great deluge.

Of the Asiatic origin of the Salmon-Eater tradition, however, there seems little doubt: laying boards across canoes lashed together— as for the wedding barge of Dzalarhons—is an Asiatic practice that exists from the Bering Sea to the China coast and on into the South Seas. Thor Heyerdahl's logical insistence that Indians of the North Pacific Coast migrated to the South Seas in ages past prompts the conjecture that descendants of such ocean voyagers later may have completed a clockwise progressive migration of the Pacific basin to return via the Aleutians to the starting place of their ancestors.

Matriarchal societies of the type characterized by both the Salmon-Eaters and the Rhaida (Haida) Grizzly Bear clan were common in northeastern Asia. These and other factors worthy of a separate volume certainly give credence to this tradition of a migrating Asiatic clan that evolved into the Northwest Coast complex of Eagle clans.

With an active maritime economy well advanced, when engulfed by the Europeans, according to known historical facts and prehistoric indications, the Indians of Totemland conveniently divide into seven main groups or "nations." (*See appendix.*) The term *nation* does not imply any centralized or organized governmental structure; it is rather a geographic means of distinguishing the linguistically and culturally related tribes who, in the days of their independence, went by a common inclusive name and exercised mutually advantageous relations.

Beginning in the Far North where totemism and the carving arts reached their zenith, the Tlingit nation extended from the Malaspina Glacier to the Portland Inlet, a prominent natural waterway just south of the British Columbia boundary. Tlingit holdings covered the breadth of Alaska's panhandle including the multitudinous offshore islands except for part of Prince of Wales Island. The Tlingit constitute the Koluschan linguistic family, and Tlingitland's southern tip is almost exactly at the historic "54° 40′ or fight" latitude that nearly provoked a third war between the United States and Great Britain. Spelled Klinkit, Kling-gate, Thlinkit, Hlingit among many variations, the Tlingit refer to Tsimsyan coastal country as their ancient homeland, a tradition conforming perfectly to the Salmon-Eater *adaorh* just related. Numbering some 8,600 according to an Imperial Russian Navy census in 1861, the Tlingit were not divided into subgroups as were the Haida and other nations but were distinguished only by slight dialectic differences. There were no major area divisions as occurred among their neighbors, the tribal structure being mainly geographic and dependent upon the lands surrounding the villages.

The Queen Charlotte Islands, an integral part of British Columbia, are the ancient home of the Haida or Hay-dah. Technically, "Haidery," as this nation was called by some of the early explorers, is loosely divided into three subgroups: the Gunghet-Haidagai (in the far south of Moresby Island and on little Anthony Island), the Haida proper or Gao-Haidagai

Old skulls like these are all that greet a casual visitor to countless deserted Indian villages. This archaeological site is in the old Haida town of Skedans (the natives called it Kona) in what are now the Queen Charlotte Islands. (British Columbia Government)

(in the largest area), and the Kaigani or Ketshade ("people of the strait"). The latter made war on the Tlingit of Prince of Wales Island, now Alaskan territory, around the year 1700 and occupied at least two-thirds of that island and several small satellite islets. Tribal organization was vague, but the clan organization was very rigid. Towns were of political importance also and, in many respects, took the place of formal tribes among these people. The total Haida population in the mid-nineteenth century stood at approximately 8,000. As an example of the tragic decline in population thereafter, the number of Haida was scarcely 600 in 1894, according to Canadian figures.

The Tsimsyan (also Tsimshian, Simpsean, Simsean, Simshean, etc.), who called themselves "the people of the Skeena," were, to be technically proper, the principal large division of the Chimmesyan nation or linguistic family. In general usage Tsimsyan has come to mean this entire nation. As one of three large related divisions called the Tsimsyan proper or Coast Tsimsyan, they lived predominantly along the coast of northwestern British Columbia, where they were divided into numerous tribes. Of the Chimmesyan nation the two other large

Fallen and forgotten totem poles like these on Anthony Island, home of the Gunghet-Haida, reflect the tragic scourge of disease and misunderstanding that decimated these people and demoralized them by destroying too abruptly the traditions of centuries. (British Columbia Government)

divisions with distinctive tribes were the related Gitksan (or Kitksan) of the upper Skeena River and the Niskae (or Niska) of the Nass River. Traditionally the Gitksan probably carried the totem-pole-carving art farther inland than any other North Pacific Coast people. The total Chimmesyan, or Tsimsyan, nation's population in the middle 1800's was about 6,500. By 1900 this number had dropped to fewer than 4,500.

Moving toward the southern portion of the region, as did the migrating tribes themselves, brings us to the Kwakiutl nation, whose traditional center is said to have been the area around modern Prince Rupert, British Columbia. When the era of European discovery dawned, however, this nation—actually one of two forming the Wakashan linguistic stock—was subdivided into three major dialectical and territorial groups: the Haisla tribes were on the northern flank, with the Heiltsuk tribes linking them with the Kwakiutl proper on the mainland and the northeast quarter of Vancouver Island. In 1900 this nation numbered roughly 2,500 people, a fraction of the population fifty years earlier.

The small Bella Coola nation was composed of several tribes distantly related by language to the Coast Salish and holding an oval-shaped territory on both sides of the river of the same name. Early Canadian government records combined the Kinisquit and Talio tribes officially designating them the "Talion nation." Actually about five tribes closely associated geographically combined for defense, since there was intermittent warfare with the southernmost Tsimsyan and considerable friction with the Kwakiutl tribes on the west and south. Their early population is not known but by 1900 fewer than 500 remained.

The other branch of the previously mentioned Wakashan language family is the Nootka, a vigorous and colorful people who held about half of Vancouver Island plus the rain-forested northwestern tip of Washington. Of the two dialectic divisions, with many tribes each, the Nootka proper was larger than the Makah-Nitinat. Whale hunting—at which they were the supreme specialists on the entire Northwest Coast—and canoe building were their distinctions. Their great, high-prowed craft of wide beam and sleek lines are credited with inspiring the design of the New England clippers. The Nootka are probably the first on the Northwest Coast to have contact with European explorers, and to trade both goods and missiles of war with the whites. At the century's turn, there were about 2,500 living Nootka.

The Salish tribes—or more correctly the Salishan linguistic family—covered the entire northern half of Washington, Idaho's panhandle, the Flathead country of Montana, and the southwest quarter (or more) of British Columbia. But *not* all of this area was part of Totemland.

The Coast Salish, though ethnically related to their kinsmen east of the Cascades, were

Indian petroglyphs on a rock wall at Sproat Lake (in Nootka country) near Alberni on Vancouver Island appear to depict a seal and a crablike figure. Petroglyphs usually indicate antiquity of habitation in the area in which they are found, and these figures would appear to predate totem poles because of the comparatively unskilled formative technique. (British Columbia Government)

part and parcel of the maritime culture and participated, though somewhat belatedly, in totemism and the coincident carving arts. There were seven distinct dialectical divisions, each having minor subdivisions and numerous tribes. Culturally they constituted a nation, in the sense previously described, and occupied the area west of the Cascades in British Columbia and Washington as follows with regard to the totem carvers: the southeast quarter of Vancouver Island and on the mainland from Bute Inlet, B.C., southward in an indistinct horizontal line running westward to the vicinity of Grays Harbor in Washington. In 1900 there were no more than 10,000 Coast Salish, less than half the population prior to white expansion.

Compressed in Coast Salish lands were at least two small groups: the Chimakuam and the tiny Quilliute nation. The former, now extinct, held an area around present Port Townsend, while the Quilliute (or Quileute) nation's main body and their Hoh division occupy a fraction of their ancient lands at La Push and Hoh River on Washington's Pacific Coast. Deserving nation status despite their small size and present number of only a few

hundred, the Quilliute speak a tongue that is distinct from all other American Indian linguistic stocks. Extremely warlike of old, they fought the Nootka-Makah and surrounding Salish tribes, and are said to have done battle with early Spanish forces attempting to establish garrisons. Their tradition includes mythology similar to that of the major Totemland nations; they carved some totem poles though not of superior quality, and they were fine canoe sailors and efficient whalers. The latter skill they learned from Makah enemies.

What made these maritime aborigines tick? A stimulating but relatively mild climate, a plentiful and easily obtained food supply, and much leisure time which enabled them to develop construction and art skills to an admirable extent. They had their barbaric side, too—what nation has not passed through such a phase? But as we approach their historical period, occasioned by European explorations, we find their mode of living and art skills more advanced than is generally realized or admitted. Even the early explorers saw their carved totem figures and marveled at their ingenuity.

2

The First European
Explorers in Totemland

The dawn of recorded Pacific Northwest history occurred in 1592 when a Greek sea captain, Apostolos Valerianus, discovered the legendary Straits of Anian, which lead eastward from the peaceful ocean into what was once called the North Sea.

Musty royal archives in Madrid tell of this voyage a century after the more illustrious but vaguer discoveries of Christopher Columbus. As the latter was alien to the Spanish monarch he served, so was Valerianus, who was sponsored by the same monarch through the offices of the Viceroy of Mexico. The Greek navigator went down in history as Juan de Fuca, the straits he discovered have long borne his adopted name, and he planted the ensign of New Spain in the vicinity of modern Port Angeles, Washington. Unfortunately De Fuca reported little of historic value with regard to the natives of the region, but Spain sought to base eventual territorial claims on his discoveries.

Two centuries later, in 1790, Don Francisco Eliza, another captain of Castille, was in command of a Spanish garrison at Nootka on Vancouver Island. On Don Francisco's orders, Lieutenant Fidalgo erected a fort and other buildings at Neah Bay, where the Nootka tribe of Makah still resides today. Fidalgo also gave his name to an important island in Puget Sound. Don Francisco also founded a tiny settlement that he named Puerto de Nuestra Señora de los Angeles. During the intervening years this expanding townsite has worn many labels. Early postal authorities were often confused by letters addressed to Los Angeles, Washington, and, in the United States census of 1860 it was called Cherbourg. Two years later, with American settlers pouring into the area, President Abraham Lincoln officially proclaimed the growing port "the second national city" and plans were initiated to make it a Pacific Coast bastion and the administrative supplement to Washington, D.C. The longer-

19

than-foreseen Civil War prevented the implementing of this ambitious program, however. The town of many names is now the city of Port Angeles.

Even before this southern portion of old Totemland came under the Stars and Stripes, though, other European powers were contending for the verdant region.

In 1741, Vitus Bering, a Dane in the naval service of Russia's Peter the Great, sailed eastward from Petropavlovsk in Kamchatka and landed on Kayak Island. Shaped like the little Eskimo skin-covered boat, this island lies close by the Alaska mainland about one hundred miles west of Malaspina Glacier. Bering, who had been striving to establish a base in Alaska since 1725, never reported his success. Shipwrecked during the return voyage, he fell ill and died, but his crew managed to return to Siberia, where their glowing reports excited the Czar's officials. As a matter of fact some vague reports hold that Bering's easternmost landfall was on Baranof Island, where stands modern Sitka—well inside Tlingit domains. Quite possibly Bering did reach this area, for his report mentioned that a small boat sent ashore never returned; he also admits sailing away when a fleet of war canoes put out and proceeded, as if to attack, in his direction. Nearly six decades later, when Baranof's Russians were foolish enough to tell the local Tlingits they had come to rule, they experienced the war skills of the natives on several occasions.

When Bering's survivors finally reached Siberia, their tales of the fur-rich region prompted new Imperial Russian colonizing efforts, and in 1783 Czarist banners flew over Kodiak Island and the plunder of the furs of southeast Alaska began. From here on dates became jumbled with the clashing interests of European powers, culminating, in 1867, with the realization of the "manifest destiny" of the United States.

England's great admiral, Sir Francis Drake, may well have preceded Juan de Fuca to this region. Drake left his name on a bay, erected a bronze marker, and first planted the British flag on the California coast just north of San Francisco (this is a confirmed historical fact), and there are indications that he cruised the Washington coast and farther north in 1578 and 1579. On the other hand, the frequency of words and names with a Scandinavian ring—in the lore of the Alaskan peninsula and in the upper reaches of Totemland—raises serious conjecture as to the possibility that adventurous souls from the Vineland colony struck even farther westward across northern Canada.

The sea trade of Europe with the mandarins of ancient Cathay and throughout the South Seas, however, caused the Czar of all the Russias also to yearn for colonies in the New World.

Spain, jealous of the territorial integrity of her North American colonies, began to move into "Alta California" as rumors spread of Russian activities in the North Pacific after Bering's probing voyages. So Captain Maurelle went farther northward than any other Spaniard had previously sailed and in 1775 he reconnoitered southeast Alaska as far as modern Sitka, although his reports are of meager value with regard to the Totemland culture.

The next important contact—quite likely the one that most hastened the demise of the native culture—was that of the famed Captain James Cook, Royal Navy. After rediscovering the Hawaiian Islands in 1777 (the original Spanish discovery in the sixteenth century was kept secret), Cook systematically surveyed the entire coast from Oregon and continued, to the alarm of the Russians, through the Bering Sea and on into the Arctic Ocean in search of the fabled Northwest Passage. In 1778 and 1779 Cook spent some time among the Nootka, basing his operations at Nootka Sound; his journals described Nootka houses and the carved poles that he took to be "images." He traded extensively with the Nootka and their northern neighbors. Finding the Indians anxious to barter the soft sea-otter pelts and other furs for iron knives, adzes, and other implements, he reckoned his cargo would fetch a fine price in the ports of China.

Lonely sentinels are these decaying totem poles on Village Island in southeast Alaska where there was a thriving Indian community when Europeans first cast eyes upon this rich area. The short pole at the left is an excellent symbolization of the supernatural being Gunah-kah-daht holding two whales. (Alaska Travel Division)

Leaving his name on Cook's Inlet, the site of modern Anchorage, he sailed southwestward and lost his life in his second visit to Hawaii. Unfortunately the Spanish navigator Juan Perez seems to have preceded Cook at Nootka Sound (Perez called it San Lorenzo), so Cook's sojourn at Nootka was to precipitate later trouble between England and Spain.

The last two decades of the eighteenth century saw a veritable parade of European and American ships to Totemland. These years are of prime importance as to *what* these explorers and traders saw and recorded in their journals concerning the native culture.

Why?

Because there has been extremely little popular material published on the over-all culture of the Totemland region, and even this churlishly minimized the creative genius of the original inhabitants.

Some writers have gone so far as to state that totem poles were not carved until after the arrival of Europeans. This is a ridiculous assumption; the totemic arts tradition goes back untold centuries. Most of the first Europeans to contact extensively various linguistic groups (*nations,* as we are legitimately calling them) and tribes verified in their journals the established custom of carving and erecting totem poles of many types.

Captain George Dixon, in 1785–87, was active among the Haida and Tlingit whose skills in carving masks particularly impressed him. In the same year the French navigator, De la Perouse, found the always-busy Indians especially desirous of trading furs for iron implements that they sought as obvious improvements over their crude tools.

Captain John Meares, an Englishman who was well known in India and on the China Coast, had heard of Captain Cook's commercial successes among the Nootka. Sailing from the Bay of Bengal in a ship aptly named *Nootka,* Meares spent two years, 1788 and 1789, in Nootka land. To say that the aboriginal civilization amazed and intrigued him would be an understatement. In his journal, Meares told of seeing totem poles but called the interior house posts "huge idols." He admitted the Indians never worshiped the carved posts, but his report, when published in London in 1791, must have caused anguish among various missionary societies and possibly inspired later brave but poorly informed souls, once upon the scene of such alleged idolatry, to force the destruction of many fine carvings. Such organized vandalism inspired by missionaries in the last half of the nineteenth century is a matter of a record as tragic as was the psychological impact upon many Indian villages. Meares unfortunately used the wrong term in describing the Nootka totem poles; he did, however, record very enlightening descriptions of the houses built with bare hands and crude tools.

By this time the sovereignty of the United States had been established and national interest prompted the new independent nation's Federal Government to give a more or less free hand to the New England shipping lines seeking to extend their commericial perimeters. American merchant ships, consequently, began to show the flag in the North Pacific because the old colonial trade with Asia, interrupted by the Revolutionary War, had to be resumed. The British were expanding westward across Canada and had reached the Pacific, the Union Jack being carried mainly by the Hudson's Bay Company. Russia, pressing southeastward from Kodiak Island, was already searching for an advanced base. Spain, in territorial conflict with Britain and Russia, was growing weaker by the year.

It was evident that the bulk of Northwest Pacific Coast wealth would eventually fall to the nation possessing the best legal foundations to make territorial claims stick in the courts of international opinion.

With this background, the scene in Kyoquot Sound—on the ocean side of Vancouver Island some 125 miles northwest of Cape Flattery—on the foggy Christmas morning of 1791 was of significance. With the Spanish garrison at Nootka Sound, Russian ships in Queen Charlotte Sound to the north, and the British occupying the southeast end of the island, the

Stars and Stripes of the infant republic, flutter-ing over a log blockhouse called Fort Defiance must have seemed almost comic. The possibil-ity of intrigue was increased because several Nootka tribes—who had just recently become "hip" to the trade opportunities—had joined in a loose federation, numbering approximately three thousand natives, under Chief Wicanan-nish. There had been several Indian attacks against European ships, and not long before an American officer and several seamen had been killed in an organized assault, for good cause in Indian eyes.

So Captain Robert Gray, commanding the *Columbia* of Boston, was on the alert. Gray and his officers, including Robert Haswell, who commanded the sloop *Adventurer*, enter-tained a number of Nootka chiefs at a Christ-mas feast, and then arranged for peaceful trade and exploration among these head-hunt-ers of the wild coast. Their reports, along with the reports of others, of the native culture, gathered during subsequent years on the Northwest Coast, reveal totem carving and construction skills to have been well estab-lished long before the white adventurers came to trade.

After examining Nootka houses and grounds, Captain Haswell in his journal tells of "poles carved into the shape of human faces with distorted features, beasts, and imaginary animals. The frame poles [the house struc-tural posts] are usually painted."[1]

John Boit, fifth mate of the *Columbia*, refer-ring to house-front paintings and doorways wrote: "Every door you entered was in re-semblance to a human and beast's head," and with obvious references to totem poles, "carved work about their dwellings, some of which were by no means inelegant."[2]

John Hoskins, a yeoman clerk on Captain Gray's ship, also kept a detailed journal for three years and observed the use of house-

[1] From a transcript in Victoria, B.C., Provincial Archives of British Columbia.

[2] From *The Oregon Historical Quarterly*, Number XXII.

front poles in combination with the over-all architecture of the houses which, "end with pitched roofs. In front is a large post reaching above the roof neatly carved but with the most distorted figures; at the bottom is an oval or round hole which is either the mouth or the belly of some deformed object. This serves for a doorway."

These men were neither ethnologists nor anthropologists, but seamen skilled in naviga-tion and in the rude trading of the time. So it is not surprising that symbolic stylizations of animals or imaginary supernatural beings should, to them, appear "distorted" or "de-formed."

After a sojourn in the Queen Charlotte Is-lands among the Haida, the same Hoskins wrote of a village in which some totem poles stood: "I went to view two pillars . . .; they were about 40 feet in height carved in a very curious manner indeed, representing men, toads [more likely frogs], etc., the whole of which I tho't did great credit to the natural genius of these people; in one of the houses of this village the door was through the mouth of one of the before-mentioned images; in an-other was a large square pit with seats all round it." Hoskins went on to describe briefly the interior arrangements of the typical Haida large, multifamily dwelling.

A contemporary of Gray, John Bartlett, also of Boston, who traded with the Haida in 1790 to 1793 for sea-otter pelts and other skins that he sold in China, was especially impressed with a village on Graham Island. Describing a Haida house, Bartlett says, "The entrance was cut out of a large tree and carved all the way up and down. The door was made like a man's head and the passage into the house was be-tween his teeth and *was built before they knew the use of iron* [italics mine]."

The evidence thus emphasized is unmistak-able: the Haida and their neighbors certainly carved totem poles and with the crudest of implements laboriously built timber houses before they ever saw or obtained the white man's tools. Yet some modern writers have said such developments came only after the white men arrived in considerable numbers.

With regard to boards or thick, wide planks such as were used by the aborigines to sheath their houses, let's see what the French explorer Étienne Marchand reported after spending two years, 1791–92, among the Tsimsyan and Kwakiutl: "What particularly attracted the attention of the French, and well deserved to fix it, were two pictures, each of which, eight or nine feet long, by *five high*, was *composed only of two planks* put together [italics mine]."[3] Marchand gave details, also, of paints of many colors and of the skill of native artists.

Clearly this verifies the ability of the natives to hew out huge planks at least two and a half feet wide with their crude stone adzes and horn, stone, or hardwood wedges. The trees—cedars—were huge, and the splitting and cutting of planks was no mean task. Wedges for splitting were of indigenous hardwoods made harder by boiling as were war clubs, wood slats for body armor, and other artifacts.

Again we find evidence of skills the origins of which were understandably not remembered by Indians questioned around 1900 or later by researchers. By the end of the last century, after several generations of European influence, Indians could not logically be expected to confirm precisely the antiquity of the ancient arts. A disillusioned, confused, and uprooted people long out of intimate touch with "the old ways," with language difficulties obtaining then as now in some isolated places, are liable to be interpreted as saying what the interviewer imagines—or wants—him to say.

Many observers and researchers, consequently, have been led to believe that most of the carving arts began with the advent of iron tools brought by trading vessels. That these arts increased with the introduction of iron is understandable; but the quotations from the journals of early navigators certainly confirm the existence of a skillful and highly developed culture *before they knew the use of iron,* and that was "before" the native culture was shattered.

[3] Bulletin 119, Volume 2, publication of the National Museum of Canada.

Though the Spanish explored widely, they never gained prominence in trade with the natives of the Northwest Pacific Coast. Nonetheless, the observations of several of Spain's navigators are of value in further exposing the modern tendency to denigrate the old native culture. One of them, Don Pantoia, a seventeenth-century explorer, found native architecture of interest. Bulletin 119 of the National Museum of Canada quotes Pantoia as follows:

"Their houses are built of nine, ten, twelve, and up to fifteen wooden posts, on which the corresponding beams are laid. Over these are plenty of boards which protect them from the continual rains. They are of different sizes, the larger being thirty to thirty-five yards long and the fronts ten to twelve wide. Inside are some large posts on which are painted with red ochre the physiognomy of some dead *talli,* which signifies 'chief' or 'captain.' "

One Spanish navigator in particular, Don Alejandro Malaspina, fortifies the prewhite tradition of totem-pole carving in his remarkable book, *Voyage Round the World,* published long ago in Madrid. A major explorer in the extreme north of Tlingit land, Malaspina, left his name on a spectacular glacier—an ice field larger than the state of Rhode Island. In describing the native village of Yakutat, the principal seat of a large and powerful Tlingit tribe of the same name, Malaspina was especially impressed with a gigantic mortuary totem pole, at least thirty feet tall, carved in the symbolic likeness of a bear. The figure's paws held a large carved box containing the remains of a dead chief. Other mortuary poles and very tall grave houses were nearby; all were on high ground outside the village and were constructed of pine, this area being north of cedar growth. Near one "idol" as Malaspina questioningly termed the totem, was a "European hat" and miscellaneous native items including otter skins. The Yakutats had traded recently with the Russians, and the old sketches in Malaspina's book show natives clothed in furs. Malaspina's reports strengthen the belief that Totemland natives carved many poles before the white intrusion.

An officer of another ship on the Malaspina

This composite of Pacific Northwest native culture at the opening of the discovery era by Europeans shows a small dugout fleet cruising offshore with a village in background. The Bear mortuary pole and the carved grave house (right) represent like carvings seen by the Spanish explorer Malaspina when he visited the northern Tlingit village of Yakutat in 1792. Malaspina's journals and those of contemporaries dispute the modern contention that totem-pole carving did not materialize until after the appearance of the white man.

expedition was Jacinto Caamaño. Having previously surveyed much of Puget Sound (an island near Everett, Washington, and Caamaño Sound, near Princess Royal Island, British Columbia, now bear his name) Caamaño was conversant with the native customs and crafts and found them vigorously practiced in Haida land in 1792.

The next year the noted British overland explorers, Simon Fraser and Alexander Mackenzie, entered areas where whites were a curiosity. Fraser, the first to reach salt water via the great river which was named for him, reported the totem arts flourishing among the river valley's Coast Salish. Mackenzie, for whom the vast and still primitive northern Canadian interior is named, visited the Bella Coola country and reported the carved totem "posts, poles and figures were painted red and black" and that "the sculpture of these people is superior to their painting." Mackenzie was, in all probability, the first white to be in contact with the Bella Coola.

The British, as well, were getting there

"with the mostest." During the years 1793 to 1795 Captain George Vancouver reported seeing "detached totem poles" and elaborately "decorated houses" in what must have been, from the available information, in the land of the Bellabella, the northernmost of the major Kwakiutl tribes.

Many explorers and empire builders of "the old days" failed to mention totem poles or other totemic carvings. To some researchers this disproves their antiquity. Many supposedly cosmopolitan moderns, however, frequently visit a museum and see nothing but the floor and ceiling.

Early visitors to Haida land, including Captain Joseph Ingraham, skipper of the *Hope of Boston,* were struck by the garb of some of the natives: European trousers and coats. Ingraham's visit, in 1791, followed that of another trading vessel. But Ingraham also reported carved poles around forty feet tall and he did not seem to believe them of very recent origin. Red cedar, the most common material for such crafts in Totemland, lasts upward of sixty to seventy years; some tribes farther inland claim poles will last around two hundred years.

The closing years of the eighteenth century were those of massive European impact upon the hospitable Indians of the Northwest Pacific Coast. By the turn of the century Captain Vancouver had pioneered the circumnavigation of the island named for him and had discovered the Gulf of Georgia in 1792. He had also convinced the Spanish that these northern waters were not for them and by accepting their surrender of the Nootka Sound colony secured the entire island for the British crown. Spain, however, did not formally relinquish claim to the entire Oregon and Washington coasts or to Vancouver Island until 1819.

Two years later, in 1821, the Russian Czar proclaimed a ukase claiming everything north of the 51st parallel, the invisible line running just north of Vancouver Island. This action by the absentee would-be landlord of Muskovy helped bring on the Monroe Doctrine two years later. The new American republic's next big territorial problem in Totemland was the "54° 40′ or fight" fuss with England over everything south of 54 degrees and 40 minutes North Latitude, the point where—on the coast—Britain had managed to check the Russians in the Alaska panhandle.

Meanwhile, down on the California ranchos, the Spanish had lost out completely to the newly independent Mexican republic, which was trying to discover a way to thwart the expansion of the Russian colony at Fort Ross some fifty miles up the coast from San Francisco. Finally a Swiss adventurer, Sutter, solved this problem, and shortly Uncle Sam, in the person of John C. Frémont, resolved everything with the help of American settlers and a flag with a bear in the middle and "California Republic" sewed beneath.

Russia had employed her customary gentle tactics in dealing with the natives of Alaska, including the Totemland Tlingits: the natives were oppressed, defeated, and ravaged by the Czar's imperial *kommissars,* but they fought back.

Not only were Totemland Indians courageous; the weight of evidence in explorers' journals, and the native traditions, credit them also with more than enough skill and originality to have developed their plastic arts well in advance of European exploration and colonization. The native standard of living and aboriginal economy will strengthen this conclusion as we examine the most unique and individualistic way of life in pre-Columbian North America.

3

Homes and Crafts,
Economy and Social Organization

*"Ye say that all have passed away—
That noble race and brave . . .
But that their name is on your waters—
Ye may not wash it out."*

From "Indian Names,"
by Lydia Huntley Sigourney

Food, shelter, and clothing are the essential requirements of all people and in that order. How well aborigines anywhere fulfill these basic needs depends upon several factors, environment and social organization being the most important. The former supplies the raw materials from which the three basic needs are obtained while the latter either encourages the development of a relatively affluent material culture or inhibits creative activity. In a larger sense, these two prime factors are interdependent.

To appreciate fully the comparatively superior level of civilization the Indians of To-

temland had already achieved prior to the arrival of Europeans, we must examine the rudiments of their culture. Just as Captain John Bartlett of Boston was amazed to find architectural skills highly developed "before they knew the use of iron," our sophisticated generation finds the Pacific Northwest Coast Indian way of life somewhat paradoxical. Though primitive in comparison to our present culture, these maritime Indians were downright remarkable for the variety of mechanical skills well established throughout the region. The only Amerind societies with such extensive architecture were a few of the Eastern woodland tribes and the Taensa-Natchez of the lower Mississippi valley region, where the structural arts were progressing toward the level attained in the far Northwest. Totemland Indians were engineers, in a manner of speaking, not diggers or shapers of mud.

The native towns which the first Europeans found were invariably situated around river outlets and along the shores of salt-water bays, the houses being conveniently placed on a rising shore a hundred feet or so above high-tide line. With the entrances facing the water, the houses were arranged advantageously with regard to shelter from the elements by the ever-present forests and geographical terrain. Usually there was a single line of houses—straight or on an arc, depending upon the shoreline—although occasionally there were two or more rows of dwellings, seldom more than twenty feet apart. A town or village was composed of any number of houses, sometimes thirty or more. Anywhere from a dozen to a hundred persons might occupy a single dwelling—a basic family to a fairly complete lineage group—and, consequently, the population of a Northwest Coast native town could easily number well over one thousand persons.

The actual ownership of each house was vested in the family or lineage head, the house chief, although the effective ownership was usually the entire family. The "house" property included the forefront area to the water line; this "beach front" was the front yard and parking lot for the house canoes. The space between the houses, less clearly defined, was also family property, though shared with the adjacent neighbor. Nearby high ground, especially when overlooking the sea in the farther north portion of the region, was often a burial area for priests and medicine men. House members below chief rank were ordinarily buried in the ground, in a box, in a tree, and less frequently in caves some distance from the village in a wooded area. The remains of chiefs and related persons of status in the North were often interred in "mortuary poles" near the houses. In the southern area around Vancouver Island all, or most, of the dead were laid to rest away from the immediate village area.

Due to a vigorous way of life, warfare was a constant threat from nearby related tribes or "opposite" clans or from distant raiding parties. Fortifications, therefore, were a necessity. Hills or rocks, if strategically located around the townsites or even in the harbor near the shore, were strong points. When attack was imminent, mothers and children were hustled to the tops of such redoubts by notched logs which served as ladders. Here they were defended by picked warriors. The main body of warriors would defend the village from a suitable perimeter, from their canoes on the water, and house by house as well. Weapons included crafted items and boulders and rocks shoved and hurled from redoubts.

The techniques of house construction varied slightly throughout the region. The Haida were probably the most accomplished builders, at least in the prehistoric period. Due to the extensive maritime travels universally customary on trade and war expeditions, however, the principal variations in dwellings were mainly the size when history dawned less than four hundred years ago. The Haida were the most widely traveled of all Totemland peoples and, consequently, their early architecture spread far and wide, and also benefited from what they observed in the domains of their neighbors to the north, on the mainland to the east, and in the southern areas.

The four corner posts were stripped of bark, generally left round, and, after being set in the ground, were cut or notched at the bottoms to accommodate horizontal side and front plates. The latter were large timbers split from huge logs of the desired length and rudely, albeit efficiently, squared off by laborious work with the adz. The sizes of houses were as much as 100 feet long and fifty to sixty feet wide, depending upon the wealth of the owner and his lineage. In general, the southern houses were larger than those in the north.

In the northern areas the roofs were invariably double-pitch or steeply gabled. This required two centrally situated vertical posts spaced four feet or so apart at the front and rear between the corner posts. These central posts, taller than the corner posts, allowed for an entrance in front and for the universally solid wall at the rear. The northern houses customarily had, in front, a special tall house-front

All that remained in the 1950's of a Haida house at Tanu in the Queen Charlotte Islands were these rotting roof support posts and beams. This appears to have been a large multifamily dwelling. The frame outline of a smoke hole can be seen. (British Columbia Government)

pole in which was cut a rather wide but low entrance. In the southern area the roofs were less steeply pitched. Roof-support plates were notched to these posts, front and rear, and centered on them was a ridgepole running the full length· of the house. Occasionally the ridgepole was hollowed to catch rain water for use by the occupants.

In recent years some have questioned the native ability, without knowledge of the wheel as such, to hoist a hundred-foot pole, for example, into place. The solution, though admittedly not a chore for weaklings, was a vari-

ation of the post-and-tackle system employed in most Stone Age cultures. The corner posts and the central pair were used as hoist points and the ridgepoles and longitudinal side frame and roof plates were positioned with roughly the same technique as was employed to erect totem poles.

In the case of the generally smaller northern area houses, which averaged around thirty by forty-five feet, the four corner posts and four central posts, paired front and rear, sufficed to frame the house. Farther south additional posts were placed in the interior and along the

A relatively small dwelling of a type occupied by a single family group (unlike that of the usual large Northwest Coast native house) is illustrated above. Corner posts were logs set upright in holes; ridgepole and roof members were adz-hewn as were the vertically secured wallboards; bark was used for the roof.

sides as required, sometimes as many as a dozen. The notched ground and roof side-supporting timbers were supplemented with lighter weight but equally long members between the front and rear roof plates. The roofs were a series of overlapping rough-hewn boards in most cases; at other times great sheets of bark formed the roof surfaces.

Each family group to occupy such a dwelling would have its own fire pit inside; smoke

outlet holes were provided in the roof boards, and other boards were usually left on the roof in order to cover these holes during rainstorms.

The house sides were formed of boards laid horizontally, one on top of the other, or positioned side by side vertically, and tied in place with tough spruce roots or ropes woven of shredded cedar bark. These side and front walls, though strong, could be employed as emergency exits or passages through which the body of a deceased person could be passed. By this means the dreaded "ghosts" of the dead were confused and could not easily wend their way back to haunt survivors or contaminate the habitations of the living.

The interiors of the houses, large or small, were as ingenious as their exteriors. The journals of Captains Vancouver, Cook, Malaspina, and others combine to provide a clear indication of the love of space and comfort, as do the recollections of elderly Indians of the campfire accounts of "the old days."

The larger the house, the more elaborate the interior. Entering the typical dwelling through the front (there was only one aperture that served as both entrance and exit) the visitor found himself on a floor of planks laid upon leveled ground. Running lengthwise, and occupying a fourth to a third of the interior width, was the fire and cooking area a foot or so lower, giving the interior something of a covered courtyard look. On all four sides, integral with and on the same level as the entry, was a ramp or "grade" similarly planked. In extremely large houses there was often an additional level or two several feet wide; these served as convenient storage places for the ever-present carved wooden boxes of all sizes that housed all sorts of personal belongings, blankets, and other valuables. Occasionally, where interior horizontal beams were needed, these were elaborately carved.

At the extreme rear of the house was the chief's private apartment secluded from view by a screen of boards painted with personal

This 1890 photograph of a chief's house of the warlike Chilkat tribe shows the interior of a traditional Totemland house, in which all space was used. In one raid upon a northern Haida village, the leather apron (bottom left) was part of the loot. The design so appealed to the chief that he ordered the women of his extended family to reproduce the symbols in woven goat wool. Thus the famed Chilkat robe—misnamed blanket—was born. The boxes in the photograph are not piled one on top of another but rest on the "grades" that surround the central lower level on which each family living in the house had its own individual fire. (Winter & Pond)

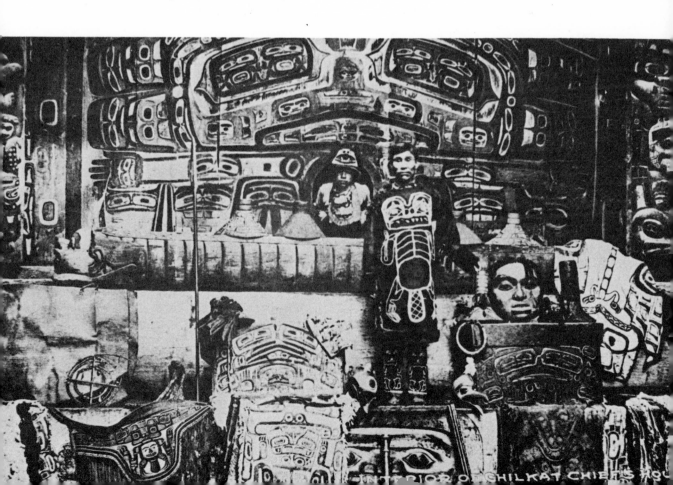

At the turn of the century the natives of southeast Alaska were still living on their ancestral village sites but in modernized houses. Totem poles still faced the waterfront and canoes were the principal mode of transportation. This is Howkan, a Kaigani-Haida town on Long Island, a satellite of Prince of Wales Island, as it looked about 1900. (Winter & Pond)

crests and other totemic symbols. In effect a "holy-of-holies," the chief's quarters were off-limits to other house occupants unless they were personally invited to enter. The interior roof supporting posts were also carved with totem figures. The uppermost level, or grade, along each side of the house was subdivided into separate and privately walled living quarters for each basic family group, all of which were in the lineage of the house owner (the chief), that of his wife, or both. Leisure hours and ceremonial occasions found these grades occupied by scores of Indians, family and guests alike. Persons of high rank, of course, were quartered toward the rear of the house. Sitting on the grades was made easier by spreading woven cedar-bark mats or furs with

wooden backrests; the latter made these levels extremely long divans, of a sort, as required.

Chiefs of particularly high rank and wealth often had a broad extension of the top grade immediately in front of the screen that walled off the royal apartment. Useful as a stage, this platform was the locale of elaborate dramas portraying real and legendary events. In a few of the restored "community houses" in Southeast Alaska today, these age-old dramas are still performed in front of duplications of the painted board screens of old-time chiefs.

Where houses were built upon a system of raised pilings because of unusually steep banks, some chiefs went all out with facilities for high drama. The stage, built over steeply sloping ground, was fitted with trap doors

LEFT: *Here is another neighborhood in old Howkan, about 1900. The American-style houses, while rectangular, were often two-storied to provide the customary interior space, whereas the ancient sprawling dwellings were one story only. Note the symbol Raven is at the top of the pole, an obviously old one as attested to by the props. Over the nearest doorway is Eagle in a style influenced by the new association with Uncle Sam.* RIGHT: *Of the same period is this house in the Tlingit town of Stikines (near Stikines Glacier). It belonged to Chief Kad-a-shan, whose ancestors were important Haida. These poles connect the family of Kad-a-shan with the family of the Tlingit Chief Shaiks. The totem symbols combine Raven when he brought light with Gunah-kah-daht. (Both: Winter & Pond)*

The lumber is comparatively smooth and cut in the modern way and the roof is covered with long cedar shakes; otherwise this Tlingit ceremonial house at Totem Bight near Ketchikan is a close approximation of the traditional aboriginal abodes. The two short poles depict Indians happily contemplating a potlatch. They are wearing the familiar spruce-root hat symbols. The house-front entry pole is dominated by Raven (top). Beneath it (fourth figure from top) is Gunah-kah-daht holding a whale. (Pacific Northern Airlines)

through which fierce fabricated spirit creatures were thrust at the climax of ceremonials. All of these remarkable aboriginal houses were of but a single story. (By the middle of the nineteenth century the press of space prompted many chiefs to build multiple-story dwellings with glass windows and much of the paraphernalia of white civilization.) Customarily the fronts of the houses were painted with totemic symbols that, together with the house-front pole, identified the clan and family lineage of the house owner.

The social system, as the preceding suggests, was on the complex side. In essence the social organization was of two distinct types: matrilineal and patrilineal with occasional scattered combinations. Here the regionally important clan system enters the picture.

Among the Tlingit, Haida, Tsimsyan, and the northernmost Kwakiutl (the Haisla), the matrilineal relationship or legal aspect of descent prevailed. The children of a basic family unit acquired their rights, names, and privileges from their mother's side of the family. Each Haida tribe or subdivision was automatically halved, by birth, into moieties. When the children reached maturity, they could marry only into the "opposite" moiety. It follows, then, that a chief's rank and titles would be inherited by his nephew rather than his son. In other words, the next in line for the chief's mantle would be the oldest son of the oldest brother of the chief's wife.

Such a matrilineal descendancy was calculated to insure a direct blood relationship with the real or theoretical ancestor, in the latter case the supernatural being who took on human form and founded the genealogical line. In Haida land a Raven man found his bride among the Eagles and vice versa. By the same reckoning the rights to specific totem symbols and crests, certain dances, ceremonial duties, and frequently valued professions such as totem-pole carving or canoe building were passed from one generation to another. In general, such a social unit was largely independent insofar as political rights and responsibilities were concerned. These rights included ownership of certain fishing and hunting areas, berry-picking plots, forest timber areas, military alliances, and the like. The importance of such descent—or clans—will become more obvious as we delve more deeply into this region's totemic or heraldic lore. In the northern nations, the Tlingit and Tsimsyan had no "halves" or moieties but four or more clans that corresponded roughly to the Haida custom.

In the Indians' ceremony-filled lives, the complications such a system spawned were multitudinous. For example, the sons and daughters of a northern chief belonged to their mother's clan lineage. Hence, in ceremonies celebrating their father's lineage, they had markedly secondary roles—and rights—when compared with their cousins who were the children of their father's brothers and sisters. By the same token when their mother's lineage was holding special events, they found themselves outranking their "opposite" cousins who had lorded it over them on a previous occasion. To analyze the complete system would require a volume in itself.

These social restrictions meant that one usually married within one's class. Divorce was generally frowned upon except in cases of adultery when there were specialized, and sometimes partially secret, rituals to be performed with picked witnesses. When one's mate died, the survivor blackened his or her face, leaving only the eyelids unpainted. After the prescribed time—several years under certain circumstances—the mourner returned to society, gave a feast, distributed gifts, and announced his or her availability for marriage again.

While sharing the mechanical arts and overall material culture of their northern neighbors the Heiltsuk and southern Kwakiutl, the Bella Coola, all or most of the Nootka, and the Coast Salish north of Puget Sound had an entirely different and often more confusing social system. Predominantly these "nations"— or, in the case of the divided Kwakiutl, portions of a linguistic nation-group—had no genealogical lineages or clans but determined descent through both the female and male line, the latter being slightly more important.

A theoretical exception to this southern pattern of custom existed among some of the Kwakiutl tribes around the northernmost tip of Vancouver Island and on the mainland where the Xaihais and Bellabella (*not* to be confused with the Bella Coola) developed hereditary subdivisions with clanlike names. Very probably this became customary because of their proximity to and coincident cultural contacts with the Tsimsyan and Haida. Children of Bellabella and Xaihais-Kwakiutl tribal couples were ceremonially designated as belonging to the father's or mother's clan as conditions of inheritance seemed to indicate. There were no prohibitions on marriages between children of these groups. Around Puget Sound and on the Olympic Peninsula the bilateral system undoubtedly prevailed anciently although precise genealogical data does not exist.

Lacking clan lineages in the technical sense, these southern-area Indians did approximate the more northern customs in that property rights, ownership of crests and hunting and fishing grounds, ceremonial duties, political prerogatives, and so forth, were passed down through a system of extended families or a group of blood-related and marriage-connected relatives. Hereditary chieftanships were held in a way essentially similar to that of the northerners except that the oldest son of a chief could inherit his father's rank and authority.

In both areas of the region the author calls

Totemland, the chief was the final ruling authority in his group and domain. He presided over the elders in council, ruled on all matters relating to war, and decided when to make a seasonal move to fishing and hunting areas, whether to engage in trade with a neighboring village, clan, or tribe, and whether the resources at his disposal were sufficient to have a totem pole carved and how much to spend on the required potlatch. In some instances women became chiefs.

If there were practical differences between the two areas, they were mainly in regard to the way in which wealth was held and used. In the northern nations hereditary rank brought automatic respect and honor—at least in theory—while among the southern nations wealth was about equal to heredity insofar as assuring status.

After Juan de Fuca's explorations came the slow process of European colonization, and the status achieved by wealth alone eventually displaced heredity and ability. This was illustrated late in the last century by the wasteful destruction of valuables in Kwakiutl potlatches, and among the declining Haida by the substitution of the white man's products like broad expanses of concrete paving in front of houses previously decorated with the magnificent totem poles of "the old days."

Everywhere in Totemland there were three principal classes of people: the chiefs, the noblemen, and the commoners. The highest ranking chief in a town, clan, or tribe would be the high or head chief of such a group. The nobility was made up of those closely related to the chief and they were regarded as persons of influence and wisdom. Commoners were comparable to their counterparts in modern monarchies. Medicine men, aboriginal doctors, and shamans, as these professionals came to be called early in the historic period, were of a distinct and separate class or nonclass.

At the very bottom on the social register were the slaves. Taken as war captives in most cases, the slaves on the Northwest Coast were usually better treated than the term implies. Often they were ransomed by their relatives.

Chattels they were, but they were allowed to marry and to have a family life of their own, often in a private portion of their owner's house. However, children of such a union were also slaves and they could be traded, sold, or given away as gifts. Indications are that slaves were seldom tortured. When, however, the occasion called for a public demonstration of authority and affluence, a slave might be clubbed to death or used as the foundation upon which a house corner post was secured. On the other hand, some slaves were so highly regarded that they were loaded with sufficient material wealth to give them status in their own right. One historic Bella Coola chief is said to have given the son of his deceased slave a substantial house and other useful property. The Emancipation Proclamation made President Lincoln a hero in southeast Alaska, and to commemorate this great event, several poles were erected in his honor, slaves freed, and ceremonies held.

The economy of the region was inextricably involved with the social system and material arts and crafts. Vancouver Island natives traded dentalia shell (a tooth-shaped mollusk raked up from shallow bay waters and valued as currency) for the horns of mountain sheep that were hunted by the Tsimsyan and their neighbors. The Tlingit traded mountain-goat horn to the Haida for red-cedar logs. The Nootka, the only regional nation that hunted whale in large numbers, dealt in the bones and oil of that great creature. The Tsimsyan held the best areas for the valuable eulachon, or candlefish, so-called because this oily smeltlike fish was dried and burned like a candle in special stone dishes. The Tlingit obtained raw copper in limited quantities and traded it far and wide; crude knives were hammered from it as were the great shieldlike ceremonial "coppers." All Totemland folk were natural-born freetraders for everything, even abalone shell from distant California.

Aside from their houses, the greatest product achievement of these Indians was their skill at canoe making. The Nootka were superior in this regard and their great craft could safely negotiate the coastal seas on voyages as far as Puget Sound and even northern California on slave raids.

When a proper tree was found—always red cedar—it was felled by stone axes or, if it was a large tree, by fire. By skillfully controlling fire with water and using stone ax, adz, and hammer, the log was shaped and hollowed. To increase beam and seaworthiness, the canoe was elevated on rocks open side up and filled with water. Red hot rocks were then placed inside. The boiling water softened the wood fibers and the gunwales were then carefully spread farther apart. Adzed flat boards placed between the sides were secured by sewing with tough roots and animal sinews. These canoe spreaders simultaneously widened the craft and served as seats. The graceful high prows and stern pieces were separate carvings secured by pegs and sewing. Adjacent tribes used the Nootka canoe that inspired several variations throughout the region. In the Far North and elsewhere small river dugouts were made for shallow waters, the shovel-nose canoe being especially popular on inland waters. In the north particularly, dugouts were painted with a myriad of symbols, as were paddles. The latter as well as the canoes were often smoothed with sharkskin. To waterproof them they were coated inside and out with grease and to complete their long-range utility, specially shaped boxes were made to fit snugly in the stern and bow sections—fitted luggage, if you please, centuries before Detroit and travel agencies and outfitters.

Salmon, several species, were the main staple food all over Totemland and were taken by spears with single or multiple prongs, by dip nets, and by damlike traps placed in the hundreds of small streams during the annual runs. Halibut, the secondary food fish, was taken by barbed hooks made of hardwood and bone splinters. When one of these large flat fish was landed, it was almost a ritual to club it motionless. Clubs for such purpose were often made of wild crabapple, or other hardwood, boiled to make it even harder. The

The warriors of Totemland were as well armed and as well protected from a contemporary's violence as were the soldiers of Europe during the Middle Ages. Wood-slat body armor, crude but effective knives or spears, hardened wooden clubs with totem carvings earned these regional warriors the grudging respect of several European ship crews who miscalculated an initial welcome as an indication of weakness.

LDSutton

Many isolated streams still provide food fish for numerous present Indian villages in the ancient lands of the Northwest Coast. Salmon-drying racks today look much as they did when "Raven brought light to the world" near the mouth of the Nass River, the traditional Eden of the three northernmost nations. (British Columbia Government)

A few dugout canoes, especially shallow-draft utility types such as these long ones with wide beams made by the Bella Coola, are still used in old Totemland. Seldom, however, can one find a canoe of the high prow and stern type or one with carvings in the ancient tradition. (British Columbia Government)

Coast Salish Indians still fish the Fraser River much as their ancestors did—with the multipronged salmon spear and the accompanying dip net. Were it not for the modern clothing, this scene could have been one of a hundred years ago. (British Columbia Government)

clubs, delicately carved and highly valued, served a dual purpose as war weapons.

Craft skills were extended also to the fabrication of body armor. As bows were made of yew or serviceberry wood, so were a series of foot-long slats. Sewed together for jackets—and reportedly for skirts as well—such primitive body armor worn over tough elk or moose-hide vests was, in battle, far better than nothing. Arrows were made of straight-grained red cedar—still the best shaft material in modern archery. In battle or on the hunt the Northwest Coast warrior showed his likely Asiatic origin; he held his bow horizontally in a manner unusual for an Amerind. Some accounts have stated that the Totemland warrior used wooden helmets with visors, despite the regional preference for masks of the forehead type. Some ceremonial masks covered the face, however, so possible links with Asia could have influenced warriors toward wooden facial armor similar to that of ancient feudal Japan.

On only a few occasions did these Indians wage an organized military campaign against Europeans. The most studied military operation was against the Russians who, under Alexander Baranof, had previously mistreated the Aleuts. The Sitka-area Tlingit finally determined shortly after 1800 to teach the manager of the Russian-American Company and his "colonists" a lesson despite the formidable fortifications defended by Imperial Navy sloops, field guns, and muskets. Tlingit women had been systematically ravaged, men taken at gunpoint, enslaved and transported in chains to a prison camp on Kodiak Island.

Kaltean, head chief of the Tlingit on Baranof Island, gathered several hundred warriors, who, armed with spears, clubs, bows and arrows, and a handful of old trade muskets, handed the Russians the worst defeat any Europeans ever suffered in Totemland. A restored old totem pole commemorates this victory which, after many days' fighting, left unknown hundreds of casualties.

Kaltean's forces assaulted the unique six-sided Russian blockhouses and well-defended stockades of Fort St. Mikhail from land while simultaneously mounting a daring canoe operation from the sea.

These Far North Tlingit had no easily carved red cedar; consequently when they could not import it, most of their dugouts were low-prowed, sleek, smaller, and carried fewer warriors. Their ancient weaponry, like that of their neighboring nations, included hardwood spears with stone, bone, slate, or crude copper tips, the aforementioned clubs, and occasional shields for close hand combat—hardened boards carved with crests and various totem symbols. In the southern area the Nootka, in canoe warfare, used all these weapons, plus whaling harpoons. Some of the Tsimsyan and neighboring mainland Indians made bows nearly five feet long with extremely stout sinew strings capable of hurling long and heavily barbed arrows.

In tribal conflict, the warlike Kaigani-Haida wrested over half of Prince of Wales Island from the southern Tlingit in early historic times, while their Gunghet cousins to the south fought repeatedly with the Kwakiutl, Nootka, and Salish on trade and slave raids deep into Puget Sound. All of these groups sought, without success, to subdue the wily Quilliute on the Washington seacoast; the latter, holding their own, even challenged the Makah-Nootka for possession of Tatooch Island off Cape Flattery.

There were several brief but serious encounters with Americans and British. One Yankee seaman, John Jewitt, was a Nootka slave for three years after his ship was burned to the water line. Captain John Kendrick, an erratically sour type who previously had traded with the Haida, once miscalculated and in June, 1791, seized two Gunghet chiefs, Koyah and Skulkinans of Anthony Island, locking them in a gun carriage on the deck of the *Lady Washington* of Boston. The chiefs, true to the "gifting" custom of the region, had casually picked up a few uncovered trinkets during a visit to the vessel with their wives and entourage. The attack that ensued a few days later—following the public disgracing of

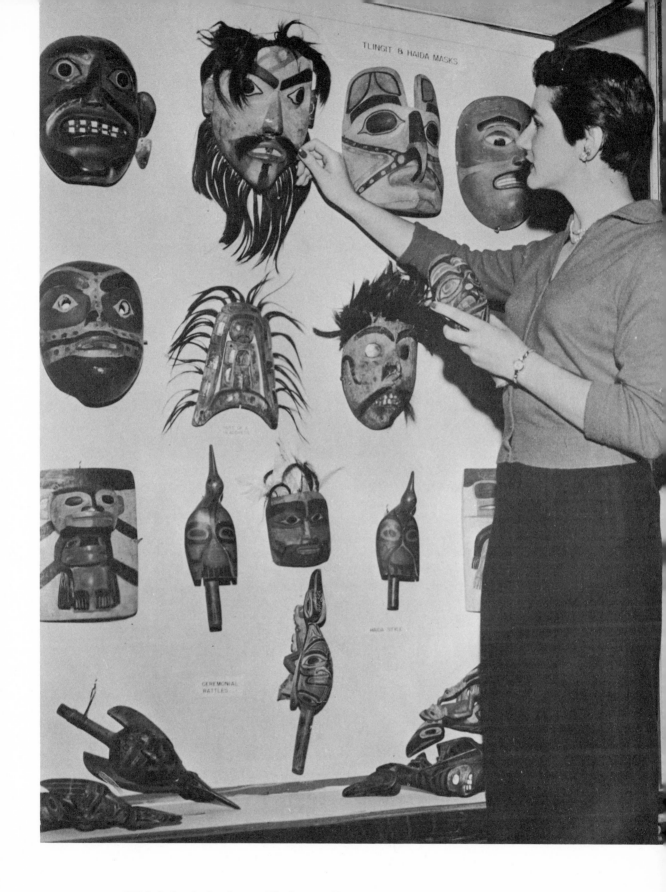

With little doubt the world's finest collection of Tlingit and Haida ceremonial masks and rattles is in the Alaska State Museum in Juneau. Haida masks tend to fit the face, while those of the Tlingit are often rectangular or pyramidal for forehead wear. (Pacific Northern Airlines)

their chiefs—included a well-planned canoe assault. Due to superior weapons there were no white losses, but a chief's wife lost an arm to an American cutlass, and musket balls and cannon grape took about sixty Indian lives.

The humiliated Chief Koyah went on a face-saving rampage. Making war on the powerful Moresby Island high chief, Skidegate, Koyah gradually regained his power and defeated the crews of two more trading vessels. All told, in the twenty years before 1805, there were at least ten known attacks on trading vessels by the Haida alone, during which the Indians occasionally managed to capture, sack, and destroy the ships. Koyah mounted assaults with up to forty dugouts carrying more than three hundred warriors. In June, 1795, when attacking the *Union* of Boston under Captain John Boit, Koyah was killed along with several other chiefs and approximately seventy warriors.

Such attacks generally opened with a hail of arrows from canoes, followed by club-and-knife-wielding warriors climbing anchor chains and attempting to fire the rigging. First contacts always saw the Indians welcoming newcomers with proffers of friendship and gifts, but when the Indians, without invitation, took a few trinkets in return as was the regional custom, slaughter invariably followed. No Totemland Indians took scalps from live enemies. If they took anything, it was the entire head. Occasionally the scalp was removed later for evidence of prowess in battle. Russians apparently precipitated the first atrocities in the north, the Spanish in the south. When the Americans and British finally arrived, they made the error of assessing "pilfering" as gross thievery and havoc followed. Some ship captains shelled and destroyed entire villages, although most records indicate they did pay the natives fairly for their sea-otter pelts and sealskins.

On the brighter side, the Indians soon learned that the white man's penchant for trinkets was as insatiable as his own. The result was the miniaturizing of their tall totem poles, and here Haida craftsmen were su-

Spruce roots were favored for basketry by the Haida, Tlingit, and Tsimsyan. These two baskets and the traditional warm-season hat (left) were woven around the turn of the century. The stylization on the large basket is Wasgo, the monster Sea Wolf of Haida mythology. (Courtesy Phoebe Hearst Collection, Lowie Museum of Anthropology, University of California, Berkeley)

The northernmost peoples are skilled in the hand crafting of small artifacts of argyllite, and in carving the black horns of mountain goats. The food ladle of horn (foreground) and the two artistic tobacco pipes are Haida of the late nineteenth century. The age of the stone paint dish (at top) is unknown; it is undoubtedly quite old. (Courtesy Phoebe Hearst Collection, Lowie Museum of Anthropology, University of California, Berkeley).

A real work of native art is this Haida feast dish of argyllite over a foot in diameter, circa 1900. It is decorated with symbolizations of what appear to be Beaver (on the left) and the monster Wasgo. In the center is a man—either a chief or a noted dancer—holding rattles. (Courtesy Phoebe Hearst Collection, Lowie Museum of Anthropology, University of California, Berkeley)

preme. Near Chief Skidegate's town—a name still remaining—there was a deposit of argyllite, a black slatelike clay that was easily carved and became hard when exposed to air. By 1825, the Indians and traders having discovered that peace was possible, hundreds of argyllite artifacts, some genuine works of art, were merchandized to trading crews. The Tlingit, Tsimsyan, and the southern groups emulated the Haida, and wood rattles and masks, horn utensils, beautifully woven spruce-root baskets and hats, and some copper artifacts became popular trade items.

The food fare of the Northwest Coast, principally fish, was supplemented with an abundance of wild strawberries and literally dozens of species of wild blackberries and raspberries. Octopus, relatively small in the region, was considered a fine dish. Cooking was simple. In each family's fire were stones of various sizes which, when red-hot, were placed in thoroughly greased water-filled wooden boxes or watertight baskets. Thus were boiled chunks of salmon or halibut, shellfish, wild lettuce, onions, and several varieties of edible moss, and sometimes bear meat or an occasional mountain goat. Salmon and animal meat was also broiled, roasted, or wrapped in leaves of skunk cabbage and baked in the edge of the fire. The diet of the region lacked starch. These Indians saw no need to engage in cereal agriculture. Thus, possibly to satisfy a physiological craving, it was customary to have large bowls of eulachon and animal oils at hand for food dipping. Early explorers sometimes characterized a native meal as a "grease feast," although this institution actually was a specialized event featuring the consumption of unusually large amounts of grease. Beverages were made of wild fruit juice, a special delicacy being an alcoholic brew of juice mixed with water and eulachon oil.

There were prescribed diets for girls and boys upon reaching maturity. For a given

A ceremonial copper, hand-wrought and hand-engraved, was a highly valued personal-property item that gave its owner vastly increased stature. On this Kwakiutl totem pole the chief is holding such a valuable copper. Shown usually (and often only) on ceremonial occasions, coppers were frequently carved on poles to show wealth and prestige; they were aboriginal dollar signs.

TOP: *Indian women still hang narrow strips of succulent salmon ("squaw candy") to dry as did their ancestors. A scene similar to this one near Lillooet, British Columbia, occurs in scores of out-of-the-way Indian villages in the Pacific Northwest each year.* BOTTOM: *A staple of Indian diet today as in yesteryear is the vast variety of berries in North America. Gathered and dried, any surplus is bartered—in the upcountry at trading posts—or sold at roadside stands. (Both: British Columbia Government)*

This Kwakiutl maiden of high rank—a "princess" we may logically call her—wears a fur headpiece decorated with a rectangular piece of abalone shell and shredded cedar bark. Feathers were worn sparingly, and the cloaklike robe is trimmed with shells and paint work. The ceremonial copper has a missing corner, a common result of personal property abuse to display affluence at potlatches. (Drawing from a Smithsonian Institution photograph)

time, girls ate no fresh salmon—only dried strips from the previous year's catch—and were secluded under a grandmother's care. During puberty a girl slept in a sitting position; to lie down would defile the sleeping place. Silence to a maturing maiden was golden—rocks in her mouth prevented talking. A hood kept her from seeing the mountains when she ventured outside; the sea and land

spirits would then not be offended. As for boys about to become men, they were often briefly secluded with their uncles for counseling; they ate no portion of meat containing sinews or muscles and, in some tribes, shoulder meat was forbidden. To violate this taboo meant later failure as a hunter; one's arrows would never fly straight, and one would become lame when hunting bear or when work-

These finely carved artifacts are grease dishes for the chief's table. The dish at left—Beaver—has a distinctly Tsimsyan style. The seal figure dish at the right is most probably Kaigani-Haida from Prince of Wales Island, Alaska. (Courtesy Phoebe Hearst Collection, Lowie Museum of Anthropology, University of California, Berkeley)

Eulachon oil was an important trade product. The tribes that owned fishing grounds in which these small fish abounded usually prospered. The oil was used to light their houses, as a condiment or a delicacy, and to waterproof cooking boxes and other items. This box, circa 1800, still shows traces of its original covering of eulachon oil. The typical Haida carving symbolizes Eagle; his wings (on sides) serve as handles. (Courtesy Phoebe Hearst Collection, Lowie Museum of Anthropology, University of California, Berkeley)

THE CHILKAT BLANKET

One hundred years ago the robes—not blankets—made by the skilled Chilkat weavers of Tlingit land were eagerly sought by the white traders as well as the Indians of the Pacific Northwest. Woven from the durable wool of mountain goats, the Chilkat apron-shaped robes, with a design of totemic symbols, were used as shawls, dancing robes, and the like. Some present-day Chilkat continue to weave these robes. (Winter & Pond)

ing a mountain goat into a cul-de-sac for a close bow shot or spear thrust, and one would be a poor canoeman.

Such customs always, particularly in the matrilineal north, required the services of the opposite clan or moiety. This held true when a house was built or repaired, for assistance at birth or funeral rituals, and for the instruction or apprenticing of a youth. All such assistance was paid for in valuable goods.

Clothing ran the gamut. Men ordinarily wore as little as the weather permitted. Women were well garbed, however, and as richly as wealth and ability permitted. The skins and fur of bear, mountain goat and sheep, seal, elk, deer, and moose were used. Decorated with bear teeth, beads made of a great variety of shells, hawk and eagle claws or puffin beaks, the Totemland Indian was well dressed. Ceremonial occasions brought out the sea-otter robes, eagle-down crowns, and the Chilkat robes. Because these materials depended upon the natural supply in distinct areas, they were economic and trade factors before the whites came on the scene.

The poorest commoners and slaves could be adequately and warmly clothed with garments woven of shredded bark of red cedar in the south and yellow cedar in the north. Vegetable fibers were combined with the predominant materials already named. Puget Sound Indians were unique, regionally, in using milkweed fiber along with goat wool. Often such plebian clothes were dyed and embroidered with spruce roots and animal sinews.

Personal adornment included labrets in lower lips—the larger the device, the higher the wearer's rank—and nose ornaments. The latter were more a man's device. Combs for the ladies were made of hardwood, horn, or bone. The same simple bow drill used to strike a spark or work wood was used to decorate such items. Head flattening, which was not a painful or damaging process, was practiced among the Coast Salish as recently as 1850; the infant on the cradleboard was beautified by soft pads of shredded bark tied in place against the forehead.

Anything these Indians could find, they would use—they tried everything. The one possible exception to the above-mentioned spurning of agriculture was an occasional, and mysterious, patch of an illusive northern tobacco species in Haida country. But the pipe-smoking habit was not widespread. During the long winter evenings on the grades around the multiple house fires, singing and dancing to the accompaniment of single surface drums, reed whistles, rude flutes, and rattles filled in the time between storytelling. Secret-society members—there was a fraternity for every imaginable purpose—staged spirit dramas,

The loose, comfortable garments of the Puget Sound tribes of about 1800 are depicted on Chief Shelton's pole, erected in 1924. The late chief worked for five years on this double-sided memorial (it stands on U.S. No. 99 on the south side of Everett, Washington). Not a true totem pole, Chief Shelton's carving does most valuably preserve authentic—not symbolic—likenesses of his people.

This totem pole (foreground) was presented to the people of territorial Alaska by Chief Son-i-hat, a Kaigani-Haida chief of Kasaan, as a memorial to a Kiksadi-Tlingit village destroyed by the Russians in a pitched battle on this site in 1804. The figures on the war pole are: Bear Mother with cubs and several other clan crests including a bird (probably Raven); several Wolf symbols; Sea Otter; and Wolf. It is said the erection of this pole was the occasion of a great potlatch. The short poles are Wolf clan house posts. (Pacific Northern Airlines)

and children imitated their elders. As everywhere on earth little boys had toys, canoes and the like, and small girls played with dolls carved of wood with hair of bark or fur. The elders played, too; games of chance with gambling sticks and sleight-of-hand tricks were popular.

The social system produced demands for artifacts that made craft skills burst forth spontaneously. A materialistic society, tempered by an aboriginal transcendentalism, this culture could not be static. Its very nature encouraged daring approaching recklessness.

When the first *mamatle* and *yets-haidagai* arrived—Nootka for "white man" and Haida for "iron people," respectively—the native way of life was ready-made for an extension of trade.

In many respects the aboriginal craving for possessions was more like our own modern mores than we realize. Certainly the Totemland way of life carried within itself the seeds of its own destruction, but that's another story.

TOP: *Haida dugout canoe paddles were the work of first-class craftsmen. The stylized painting on this pre-1900 example depicts Beaver—the scaly tail is the tipoff.* BOTTOM: *Paddle styles were fairly standardized throughout Totemland. Note the untapered shank, the well-formed hand grip-hold at the end. The painted symbol on this very old Haida paddle is of a sea monster, probably the Sea Wolf Wasgo of Haida land's traditional lore. (Both: Courtesy Phoebe Hearst Collection, Lowie Museum of Anthropology, University of California, Berkeley)*

4

Religion in Totemland

Religious beliefs among the Indians of North America were similar in over-all concept. There were, however, widely diversified applications due to the specific interests and environments of the many regional groups. Indians of the totem-pole-carving area, as has been mentioned, enjoyed a pleasantly mild climate conducive to an abundance of food without the need of cultivation. Neither was extensive hunting necessary to feed the family, although animal meat and hides were used. Because there was no constant conflict with nature, they led a relatively easy life, with leisure for the contemplation of their origins and surroundings. Earth Mother was good to them and fruitful.

Partaking of nature's storehouse with such unusual ease, and vaguely aware that such bounty was not of their own making, the inhabitants of this vast area were in unison with their environment. The psyche of the Totem-

land Indian was, however, like that of primitive peoples everywhere: curious and fearful, yet in a sense trustful; respecting all living things, while out of necessity using everything available to sustain their own needs. It was both essential and, particularly in this rich region, remarkably easy to do so.

From this life of relative ease, in comparison with that of the Arctic Eskimo or the Indians of the arid Southwest, they developed a casual but sincere belief in the immortality of the inner being.

Their concept of a never-ceasing renewal of life prompted them to an areawide ritual of the first salmon. All of the sea and land creatures were considered human and, consequently, also had an "inner spirit" or soul. All creatures had shelters and villages in their own clan and tribal domains. The vague "source of all power" had endowed them, as it were, with the ability to assume various outer bodies—or garments—when they ventured abroad. (This belief permeated all aspects of their daily lives.) When a salmon, the universally most habitual daily food, was caught, its flesh served a useful purpose without taboo. However, because the "mortal part," the flesh, was thus appropriated, the creating deity, or deities, would expect the return of the immortal part upon which the creature had assumed his particular outer form.

The solemn return of the undamaged skeleton of the first salmon caught each season to its own domain, the water, allowed the immortal part to be renewed. Accomplished with incantations and reverence, this was *not* a sacrifice but a regional counterpart of the first-fruits ritual widespread among primitive agricultural races. To the Northwest Coast Indians this was as logical as the growth of a new trunk with branches from the stump of a felled tree. Unlike many other primitives, however, these Indians did not expand their ancient rituals into any formal form of worship with a prescribed and specialized location or liturgy.

For the most part, the idea of one God or an all-powerful overruling single Supreme Being was vague, though by no means lacking. There were, however, a multiplicity of divine or supernatural creatures who performed definite creative, re-creative, and managerial or teaching functions assigned by the nebulous principal God who was believed to exist but whose personality and character were unknown.

One is reminded of Saint Paul's visit to Mar's Hill as recorded in the New Testament. Perceiving the worship of the Greeks to be directed to many gods with specific areas of authority, Saint Paul addressed himself most vigorously to the people with an introductory reference about the statue erected to "the *unknown* god." All the Mediterranean peoples had a highly developed system of deities who were accorded rank from top to bottom. Undoubtedly the failure to devise a written language inhibited a comparable stratification of supernatural beings in Totemland; there they

were more or less equal in status. This is curious in view of the fact that the daily lives, individual duties, and privileges of these maritime peoples were subordinated to, and restricted by, the most rigidly enforced caste system in pre-Columbian America.

Because of the continued controversy concerning the earliest contacts from abroad—whether from Asia in the seventh or eighth centuries A.D. or from Europe in the years following Columbus' voyages—one can only surmise the possible origin of a belief in so many comparatively equal deities. If off-course seafaring Buddhist monks from China or Japan did visit the West Coast of America, as many scholars believe, it is conceivable that they left a residue of faith in a Supreme Being. The belief in life renewal, or transmigration of the soul into a new body, also contains a hint of Buddhist inspiration.

A number of tribes had a tradition of belief in one fairly supreme God. For example, some Coast Salish and adjacent Kwakiutl, Nootka, and Bella Coola tribes around the near Georgia Strait considered Khaals ("He who dwells above") as the supreme Deity and "transformer." Lesser beings also were believed to be of divine origin but subject to Khaals and related similar divinities. Elsewhere in the region the lesser supernatural beings, however, were seldom ranked in any particular order.

This widely held native belief further suggests the possibility of Asiatic visitors in prehistoric times. Supporting this theory are the several types of artifacts, native to the region, that have characteristics similar to others of Chinese, Korean, and Japanese origin. The widely used pointed hats of spruce roots are an example. Similarly, the regional absence of any pattern of mass worship suggests a remote influence of ancient, informal Buddhism. In confusing contrast, however, are the many myths of supernatural experience that have a curiously Biblical flavor.

Of a class in their own right, without the caste distinction of their brothers, were the aboriginal priests. "Medicine men" would be a better term, for their responsibilities embraced the healing of body and soul, the interpretation of the supernatural, and the appeasement of the unseen world with incantations and the familiar paraphernalia of the medicine man-sorcerer in all primitive cultures. The many semideities and the character of the guardian spirits are, in themselves, fascinating subjects.

The Tlingit *iktuh,* the Haida *s'haga,* the Kwakiutl *tsitsiqua,* were trained from childhood. In some tribes, principally in the southern section of the region, females of the proper frame of mind were as acceptable as males, although the latter predominated.

Indian tots, as soon as they could walk, were taught the tribal traditions and their own relationship to the heavenly bodies and to the flora and fauna. They learned the latter were of "two parts"—spirit and body. Devout adult Indians, those claiming protégé status of one or more of the guardian spirits, were the examples of the little ones, who followed them in their schedule of daily ritualistic bathing and purification. Mother and father had many household utensils and boxes; virtually every inch of surface on such artifacts was covered with pretty carvings and paintings. With only slight encouragement, the children would begin to recite the spirit songs and incantations employed by their elders. Imitating their parents, they would soon learn about supplication and penance—the rudiments of spirit devotion.

Precocious children—considered by the primitives to be selected by that vaguely defined Divinity—were brought to the medicine man's attention. If the shaman (a Sanskrit word meaning medicine man that drifted into the vernacular with the Russian colonial adventure in Alaska) thought the child adaptable (worthy), he would suggest fasting and prescribe specific incantations. If the child proved a bright pupil, the shaman would suggest that spirit power was upon him and that a prolonged absence from his (or her) parents would assure development of ability to command the spirits controlling sickness, health, the elements, and so forth. The economics of the region being what they were, the parents would promise to pay for the training.

Parents of low rank were particularly susceptible to such an arrangement, for not only would the child—*if* he became a shaman—be in a class without caste restrictions, but his prestige would increase immeasurably the status of his parents.

In some tribes the shaman specialized in healing sickness, which was always "caused" by either displeased supernatural beings or by witchcraft. Some shamans exercised power over all manner of situations, including peace and war. The Tlingit *iktuh* was a master of all the dark arts and, as the sorcerers they were, sometimes exceeded chiefs in power and status. Small figures and hideous devices were employed in casting or relieving spells, and sleight-of-hand enabled many of them to obtain wealth and power over entire villages. As recently as 1910, the natives of the Chilkat village of Kluk-wan trembled whenever the name of the *iktuh* Shah was spoken. Even Shah's servant, Gow-gē-a-deh, whose enormous drum struck fear to the hearts of the sick and well alike, was memorialized with his master after both had died.

Some Tlingit and Haida shamans were ranking hereditary chiefs. The power and wealth that accrued to such high-caste persons were staggering, the spiritual aspect being inherited, in such instances, along with his temporal rank.

Often the aspirant to the shaman profession found himself a mere assistant. The fear of the unseen spirit world, which his master appeared to control, was sufficient to keep him on the job of obscuring the strings and sticks that actually motivated the spirit devices. A shaman's success was dependent upon convincing the lay folk that he had received from various spirits their actual power. The distinction between one of such apparent power and a lesser person who was a mere protégé of one or more guardian spirits was that the shaman claimed to be the appointed agent of the spirits, whereas the protégé enjoyed only their protection and guidance. The shaman made a living—often quite fraudulently—from his craft, while the protégé could only call upon his tutelary spirit for assistance in his daily

The significant aspect of this preserved Tlingit grave figure from Cat Island, Alaska, is the conical-shaped spruce-root hat on the carved figure of a man. Worn since pre-historic times in Totemland, this is but one of the many signs of Oriental influence. On the deceased's head is Bear, his guardian spirit. (Pacific Northern Airlines)

tasks or in times of stress. The protégé used such "medicine," for instance, in the hunt, in selecting a tree for carving, and so on. The clothing worn by the shaman was frequently in imitation of the shape of the spirit that possessed him.

War parties never embarked without the frantic incantations and mysterious advice of a shaman who would often demand, and obtain, the command of the expedition. Courageous chiefs, however, would seldom allow such arrogance, for to do so would inevitably lead to their loss of face and ultimately require redemption in a special potlatch.

Warfare invariably offered shamans of opposing sides the opportunity to show their power: they would invoke disaster on the foe and engage in spirit battles with the sky as the battlefield. Cleverly timed by means of the weather-forecasting talents of many primitives, a sudden thunder and lightning storm, followed by a cloudburst, could be convincing evidence that the Thunderbird spirit lived in that shaman as he claimed. He could "throw" his spirit through the air to strike a foe.

As mediums or intercessors, shamans sometimes demanded that a supplicant submit to painful scarification. The penitent victim of such a physical ordeal would carry the scars with him to his grave as a constant reminder that his shaman had persuaded the unseen powers to accept such evidence of true contrition. The sinner was thus deprived of several strips of flesh but his soul had been purified, or so the shaman assured him.

In Nootka land the *uctak-u* were healers. Like healing shamans elsewhere, they employed their spirit power to withdraw disease that had been conjured on the victim by a foe. The disease might conveniently be extracted by removing insects or splinters, for example, which coincidentally happened to be on or near the affected area. The actual illness might be genuine or imagined, so great was the psychic power of some shamans.

The cause of much sickness was diagnosed frequently as "soul loss." The soul, synonymous with one's "vitality," particularly from the Bella Coola country to the south, would have to be captured or death would result. Shamans with a talent for restoring such lost souls carried boxes of tubelike devices, gadgets looking like cups, or frightful costumes enabling them to penetrate the "house of the cannibal spirit," for example, and retrieve the abducted soul. In a trance the "soul restorer" would whoop and yell, appear to fly about the house where the sick person lay. In a frenzy he would bite pieces of flesh from the limbs of the spectators and devour them. (Early investigators' reports allude to the frequent presence of accomplices, hired by the shaman, who willingly donated an ounce or two of flesh in return for a dentalia necklace or free instruction in the profession.)

Vancouver Island was the stronghold of the *si'oua*, female shamans who obtained power only after prolonged instruction from an experienced practitioner. A *si'oua* employed a "sacred tongue" in which she audibly invoked the intercession of spirits who would cause a barren woman to bear children. Charms, rattles, drums, and sometimes special masks were employed to appease the evil influences of the spirit world. It is said Mole's spirit was of assistance in such efforts.

Probably the most powerful of all spirits "possessed" by shamans was that of Dog. Particularly was this so among the Tlingit (and possibly the northernmost Haida of Prince of Wales Island, Alaska) where this spirit, in an evil mood, caused those in disfavor to lose control of their limbs. Unconsciousness sometimes resulted and only the timely services of a shaman could throw back the evil long enough for the antidote, a meal of dog flesh, to be administered.

Healing shamans employed physical means as well as alleged spirit power in curing maladies. Cures were said to be effected by blowing through pursed lips on the painful body area or sucking—as one would a rattlesnake bite. Herbs, potions, and poultices were employed for ailments similar to those for which more conventional societies have used "folk medicine." Often these natural remedies

Beside the seashore on the southwest side of Vancouver Island is this Indian cemetery adjacent to the village of Friendly Cove near Clayaquot Sound in Nootka land. Christian crosses now mingle with totem etchings on modern stone markers. (British Columbia Government)

GOW-GE-A-DEH ~ IKTUH GRAVE.

Circa 1890 is this foreboding grave figure of the feared iktuh Shah, who held his Tlingit people in subjugation by all the black arts at his command. So powerful was he that his figure was accompanied in death by that of his servant Gow-ge-a-dek (center figure) and by a representation of a deformed child (left) the iktuh had treated. (The inset at the upper left shows the shed over the shaman's grave.) (Winter & Pond)

This powerful but seldom seen symbol of Dog's guardian spirit—often summoned by Tlingit shamans—is shown on this old pole originally erected at a potlatch in Tuxekan in the territory taken in war by the Kaigani-Haida. A man is holding the limp body of a dog in his arms (top figure); Bear (underneath) is shown as a personal totem or clan crest. (Alaska Travel Division)

60 THE TOTEM POLE INDIANS

accomplished their purpose. Surgery was not used by the Northwest Coast shaman except in very minor instances.

Charms replete with totem symbols—the efficient shaman would carry a large boxful in his canoe—were rubbed on the diseased area while special incantations were recited. A trance was a handy escape from reality; the longer "one part" of the shaman was with his personal guardian spirits, the greater his fee and the more certain the victim's recovery.

In the Puget Sound area "spirit canoe boards" were a necessity for specialists in retrieving lost souls. Three or four feet long and a foot or more in width, these boards were carved with spirit symbols. (Some of the seagoing equivalents of Sasquatch, the forest monsters, used them in their mischief-making.) Wildly waved about the shaman's head as he danced, the canoe boards enabled that "one part" of him to wend its way swiftly to the lair of the offending spirit monster who was holding the soul. Ransom, of course, had to be paid by the kin of a dying victim. The lion's share of the price—we should say Mountain Lion's share, for that creature is a desirable spirit—increased the shaman's possessions.

Despite much sham and sensationalism on the part of many medicine men and priest-shamans, there are reports in various archives of what appeared to be cures of various illnesses. Some of the shamans were impostors and frauds—outright quacks such as exist today in the medical underworld—while others were considered by early pioneers—and are considered even by some present-day Indians in remote areas—to be genuinely capable of effecting cures through sincere prayer. They did provide a necessary function in orienting the laity—the more genuinely devout ones, that is—toward a personal relationship with the spiritual world.

A form of heraldry—an applied coat-of-arms, in fact—the aboriginal totem was *not* a spirit device or image to be worshiped. A totem, technically, was a type or class of object symbolizing the owner's belief that his lineage was descended, in a blood line, from a

land, air, or sea creature of supernatural origin. Totemism, consequently, is merely the serious practice of employing totems. On the Northwest Coast, contrary to popular belief among whites to this day, totem poles were *never* worshiped. They were, however, respected and revered as the only means of recording and displaying one's genealogy and events of importance.

Shamans also exorcised ghosts, by using spirit power. They officiated at funeral rites—in some tribes where their influence with the spirit world was sought, for a fee—to prevail against the departed spirit's tendency to "return to his house." If a mourner accidentally touched a dead body, the shaman immediately advised the contaminated person of the cleansing procedure to be observed: a series of purification baths, an artificially induced sweat to release the evil impurities from the body (perspiration was positive evidence of infection), and the correct incantations to repeat.

Some Indians today, in recorded instances, still send for a shaman when seriously ill. When he arrives, he cleanses his hands and by supplication and seldom translatable incantations "summons" his power. During this solemn interval an elder will persuade his clansmen to contribute the fee. "In the old days payment was in blankets, abalone-inlaid valuables, and dentalia, but now we usually pay for the medicine man's travel expenses and time with United States or Canadian money."

A shaman in recent times has said, "I shivered. My mind was concentrated on the sick man; power was already flowing into my hands; and it disturbed me to see the money."

He then related how he told the people to keep their money until the cure was assured: "I did not come here for money but to cure your chief. If I cure him, you shall always remember me and hold my name in honor."

This shaman repeated his chanting and then: "My power came back to me and I laid my hands on the patient, whose gall was spilling over into the liver. He fainted, being so weak that he was ready to die. I treated him

Near Hazelton, British Columbia, in Tsimsyan land is this Indian cemetery. The Bear Mother totem-figure grave marker, of stone in the modern manner, attests to the respect which the survivors felt for the traditions of the deceased. Such reminders of "the old days" are common on the Pacific Northwest Coast. (British Columbia Government)

for three days. On the fourth I bathed him and helped him to rise to his feet. His sickness was cured."

This case is recorded in official archives.[1] Let's hear this medicine man's final words; they are typical of a remarkable number who still follow early traditions:

"This is the way of the true medicine man. When he is treating a patient, he pays no attention to the amount of money or blankets that the people offer him; if his patient dies, he returns everything that has been given to him."

Dreams, visions, and contacts with the unseen spirit world continue and the ancient arts frequently achieve results that confound modern science.

[1] Memoir Number 2 of 1955, by Wayne Suttles, edited by Wilson Duff, British Columbia Provincial Museum, Victoria, B. C.

Numerous graveyards, to this day, display totem grave figures, some of them made of concrete and stone, and, in a synthesis of modern Christianity and ancient totem lore, shamans still have a place.

In summation, shamanism was a profession devoted to mediation with and influence upon the spirit world. There was, in essence, an approximation of "inner spirit," or soul, surrender to an unseen power. While some shamans were charlatans, others were not, as is witnessed by many Indians who have forsaken, but still respect, "the old days."

Personal religion was spirit devotion plus a systematic "search" for spirit guidance. It was a primitive outgrowth of "the inner part" that told the aborigine he was not of his own making, not of accident, but that his body had a spark of the Divine.

5

In the Beginning, Raven . . .
and Other Supernatural Beings

"In the beginning," as the elders related their genesis story, "Raven made us, and everything, and totem poles, too."

From time immemorial, the stories told of the carving of totem poles by "the people" after having received directions from supernatural beings on epic journeys, in visions or trances. Indians picking berries at the water's edge looked into the ocean depths and saw totem poles. The myth grew and a deluge—strikingly similar to the Biblical flood—nearly overwhelmed the people. A chief's son, the guest of sea spirits, saw carved poles, which he persuaded his people to duplicate upon his miraculous return to his village. At the resulting legendary potlatch, the salt water, stirred up by the sea spirits, rose so violently that all the land was submerged. Transformation, by changing skins or bodies, enabled most of the potlatch guests to escape as creatures of the air. Such transformation from one form to an-

other has the previously mentioned flavor of Buddhism. In the more southern nations, the myths describe Thunderbird as the agent of mercy, while Sea Gull and other "water birds" rescued protégés under similar and vaguely related circumstances. One cannot but be reminded of the Biblical messenger, the dove, which was Jehovah's instrument in guiding Noah to dry land.

The most attractive of all "flood" traditions to our skeptical age is that of the chief who built a great "floating house" when the sea began to cover the land in southeast Alaska. As this amazingly plausible story best illustrates the prehistoric growth of heraldry and crests by way of totemism, it is told in the next chapter as a principal guardian spirit concept still held in some esteem.

To completely document the ageless mythology of the aboriginal Northwest Coast Indians, even briefly, would require a shelf of volumes. Consequently it is imperative that any accounting of the genesis mythology relating to the Deity or supernaturals of this region be confined to the most widespread traditions.

The serious student of Asiatic culture and religions will find much of interest in the traditions of our totem-pole Indians, as will devotees of orthodox Judaism and the fundamental doctrines of Christian theology.

This brings us back to the apparent "beginning of the world" of Northwest Coast mythology, and to the genesis of religious faith and psychic experience (or imagination) influenced by nature itself.

Going back, then, we come to the extensive realm of Raven who, in an infinite number of myths, did everything, knew everything, and seemed to be everywhere at once. In fact, Raven combined the characteristics of evil and good, with the latter fortunately prevailing. Once he was so good and pure that he was all white. For his later mischief, mythology says, he was turned black forever. Through uncounted centuries the councils of the primitives of Asia and the Northwest Coast resounded with stories of the time when all was chaos. Raven, in Siberia, was the agent of the Supreme Being in bringing a semblance of order to a dark world of evil. Despite this remote Asiatic myth, we venture to the Nass River, where "Yethl" had attributes even more provocative, and reminiscent of several familiar Biblical personalities of divine as well as human origin:

We see Raven, or Yethl, in his most familiar Northwest Coast guise as "the changer" or transformer in the time when "darkness covered the face of the earth" or—as the Indians have said—"when the people had no light." Generations of Indian children learned these stories. Carvers put them on poles.

The great god-chief Nass-shikke-yahl had created all of the world's people. "Eden" was the fertile mouth of the Nass River which flows into the Pacific Ocean near the tip of Alaska's panhandle. Only one thing was wrong:

The whole world was in darkness, and men, beasts, and the sea and sky creatures—most of whom, at least, had been made by Nass-shikke-yahl—had to grope about without light. This made existence very difficult. The only remedy the people had discovered was the eulachon and, when they managed to catch enough of them, they dried and burned them in their small stone dishes and so lighted their houses.

Yethl, with great perception and compassion, decided to rectify the situation by playing a trick on the creator chief. "I will transform myself in such a way," thought Yethl, "that I will become the grandson of Nass-shikke-yahl, who is much like the people he made, and he will not be able to deny a baby boy anything he wants."

So Yethl transformed himself into a hemlock-tree needle floating on the water in the well where Nass-shikke-yahl's daughter came daily for the water for the chief's house. Yethl knew the princess always took a drink of the water. Sure enough, she took a drink and, without realizing it, swallowed Yethl.

Now this could only have happened with her father's knowledge, but the god-chief said nothing until his daughter's condition became obvious. When her father questioned her, she told him that one day while taking her customary drink of water at the well she had felt something small slip down her throat. When her time drew near, her father told his servants to prepare a bed of moss for her.

Presently the child arrived and the young mother named him after her father, the god-chief. Making a cradle from a basket, the grandfather decreed that all people would use baskets as cradles from that time on.

As the cunning Yethl had assumed, Grandfather spoiled him when he began to crawl about the house. First he begged for the Moon, which he threw high into the sky. He did the same with all Stars. Then he saw the carved wooden box containing light. (He knew all along this box contained the Sun or he would not have embarked upon this adventure.) So the creator chief said, "Bring the child to me." Then he told his namesake and

ABOVE: *The most attractive of all Raven and Sun poles is this Tlingit grave figure. On it are the Raven god Yethl holding the box containing light (Sun), Mink, and Frog. In 1902, when this photograph was taken, it stood near Ketchikan. (Winter & Pond)* RIGHT: *Now, restored with unauthentic, garish paints, it stands in Saxman, Alaska. (Alaska Travel Division)*

heir, "Now I will give you the greatest thing of all," and he gave the wonderful box containing Sun to Yethl who, of course, was in human form.

To make a long myth short, Yethl, now a sturdy young boy, went to the riverbank where the people were fishing. The people were rude and noisy, so he told them to be quiet or he would let light shine on them. Many canoes were filled with Indians, who taunted him, saying, "You are not the chief who made the world. You do not have light." The people became noisier and noisier, and Yethl knew they were all really terrified at the thought of having light shine on them.

Suddenly he opened the Sun box just a little bit. All over the world, light flashed as if there were a great lightning storm. At this the people became even more angry and frightened, so Yethl opened the Sun box lid all the way and there was light everywhere.

The foregoing beginning-of-light myth is the principal Tlingit version despite its origin being in historic Tsimsyan territory. The latter called their Raven god Trhaimsem or Wee-gy-et, which sounds similar to Wee-get-weltku, the Giant Woodpecker of the Kitwancool tribe some distance up the Skeena River in the same general area. The Haida had a Raven god, too—Choo-e-ah or Qaque. In some versions there were three boxes containing Sun, Moon, and Stars. In all these myths of the release of light, however, Raven transformed himself first, was invariably taken into a princess' body where he was conceived as of supernatural origin, though always there was a higher chief, a fisherman, or another supernatural being who was aware that this was a metamorphosis of Raven. Raven's sharp eyes always saw things others were unable to see. In another Tlingit version, he retransformed himself and, carrying the Sun box, "flew upward through the smoke hole of the head chief's house into the sky where he released the light."

In still another Tsimsyan coastal myth, Raven made the stars by smashing bits off the Moon, and, after releasing the Sun, disguised himself as a Crow woman and traveled to the ends of the world. One day he saw his reflection in the water, was disgusted with his long Crow's beak so he invented the labret by breaking off the end of his beak and placing the piece in his (or her) lower lip. This is how Crow became a crest.

Some Haida say Raven, when rearranging the previous creation so there would be light everywhere, got into trouble by stealing Moon, and then broke his long bill on a halibut hook. At other times he had the assistance of Mink and Frog. In Nootka, Bella Coola, and Kwakiutl lands, he became a fellow "rearranger" with Thunderbird and had some adventures with Hohoq.

The supernatural myth of the Bear Mother is also universal in Totemland and accounts for a taboo among the Tlingit against hunting or eating bear. The reason for this abstinence (tabooed foods are virtually unheard of elsewhere in Totemland) is that many Tlingit tribes have Bear "ancestors"; the less superstitious Indian of other nations did not feel it necessary to show his "ancestor" such reverence.

For similar reasons the Haida were extremely careful to cleanse or "purify" themselves by a sweat bath before a feast of bear meat. Having no taboo against killing a bear for food, they did, however, eat bear meat moderately in comparison with their usual custom of eating as much food as they could hold. Why? Many Haida families were also descended from supernatural Bear Mother, and to offend this guardian spirit—as Bear became—would be to court certain trouble and possibly a fatal accident.

The supernatural Grizzly-Bear-of-the-Sea (Medeegem-dzawey'aks) of the coastal or Tsimsyan proper is still a favorite story-myth in the north:

Long ago many hunters were killed because they insulted the supernatural Mountain Goat and his clan. The survivors returned to the Skeena River. There was a trout-filled lake close by. While fishing one day, an enormous supernatural Grizzly smashed the fishermen's

In Klawock Totem Park on Prince of Wales Island, Alaska, are poles of the Kaigani-Haida showing two of the principal mythical creatures. The pole at the left shows Bear (upright), with Killer Whale on his head; at right, facing away, is a restored Man creature with most high Raven on his shoulders. (Alaska Travel Division)

LEFT: *A Tlingit high chief, Shaiks, owned the fine Gunah-kah-daht pole with Killer Whale on his head (see left), which is shown here as it still stood in its original condition on Shaiks' Island near Wrangell in 1890. The sectioned fin on top is a variation of the skeels and probably referred to three potlatches Chief Shaiks had given. Supernatural Grizzly Bear (see right) is a crest pole commemorating Chief Shaiks' victorious raid on another tribe in which he took the crest by force. (Winter & Pond)* RIGHT: *The high chief's two poles as they are now preserved on Shaiks' Island. (Pacific Northern Airlines)*

cedar log raft, but was killed by spears. The fishermen recognized it as the sea-bear monster because it had human faces on its fin and long human hair. Foolishly they cut off the monster's head and tore out its claws and much of its hair. This so outraged the water spirits that they caused a foam—not real water—to flood the ground even up the mountainsides. The spirits were avenging the "Mountain Goat people" as well as Sea Grizzly. Seeking to appease the spirits, the Indians discarded first the monster's hair, then the claws, and finally the foam stopped rising and the people were safe.

Having kept the monster's head, they composed a special song and held a great feast. The people, from that time on, carved many totem poles, some of them showing Bear with Killer Whale on his head because sometimes the former had characteristics of the latter. The myth has many variations and in one form or another is a crest throughout most of Totemland.

Among the Stickine tribe of the Tlingit the most valuable of all crests are Hootz and Keet, the supernatural Grizzly and Grampus (or Killer Whale) respectively. The most outstanding southern Tlingit chiefs became a virtual dynasty, the Shaiks, of historic times. Greatly respected, this name is still held by heredity in the Wrangell area. A former Chief Shaiks went to war with another tribe and, in the settlement, won as a crest the Grizzly totem. The old chief always stoutly maintained that supernatural Grizzly often climbed the Grizzly Bear pole that stood before his home on Shaiks' Island. As the most powerful animal known on the Northwest Coast, to own Grizzly as a crest implies great personal power and influence.

The most famous, most often told, and probably the least understood mythical saga—repeated and distorted all the way south to Vancouver Island—is that of the supernatural Gunah-kah-daht. Because the Shaiks line of chiefs claimed "domination of the sea" as their "prerogative," their Gunah-kah-daht totem pole (this also stands on Shaiks' Island) is one

House-front paintings combined stylization of symbols with a technique sometimes spoken of as "X-ray." On Shaiks' Island is this painting of supernatural Grizzly Bear. The small faces symbolize both strength, or inner spirit power, and the body joints. Paintings similar to this one have been copied on tapestries and passed off as ancient Mexican-area gods. (Pacific Northern Airlines)

of the greatest poles of all types still standing.

In the dim past a chief of great power named Nah-tse-tla-neh (reduced to the duller-toned Natsilane in recent years) was far from shore hunting sea otter. A sudden storm caused him to despair of ever reaching home. He knew each moment might be his last. Then out of the thrashing waves there slowly appeared an enormous manlike figure. The supernatural giant stood almost clear of the waves a minute or so, then sank beneath the surface as slowly as he had appeared.

Nah-tse-tla-neh recognized the being as Gunah-kah-daht and remembered that whoever looked upon him would be assisted, find safety, and eventual greatness. After more hours of what would have been terror had he not seen the being, this hero's canoe was wrecked on a distant shore, but Nah-tse-tla-neh and his companions were uninjured. He and his crew searched the wooded island, found no other people, no food, and no fresh water. Had the vision of the being been a dream? Were they lost after all?

While sleeping, he was told that if he would make eight totems of the Keet (Grampus or Killer Whale), he and his men would be rescued. The miracle of all this was that the Keet was so terrible that, until this event, it was unheard of. Told that all living sea creatures would flee to the shore when he finished his eight totems and placed them in the sea, Nah-tse-tla-neh worked many days with his stone ax without food to strengthen him. Seals and fish teased him by leaping over the waves but eluded him; he and his men were starving.

Finally the totems of Keet were completed and thrown into the sea as he had been instructed. When the tide went out, the shore was covered with seals and fish frantically trying to escape the totems which had come to life. Thus rescued from starvation, the hunters were able to build a new canoe and to return home safely.

To this day when the tall dorsal fin of the Keet is seen, the people know they will have fine fishing and sealing fortunes. Though essentially evil, the Keet helps those who see the powerful Gunah-kah-daht. Other versions have the hero a henpecked, abused son-in-law who, though a bit lazy, was a great hunter of seals. He was a good provider, but he and his wife's mother fought constantly. Out of desperation he built a small house on a lake and began to search for a supernatural being said to live there. With his stone tools he cut a great yellow cedar, made a trap, caught and killed the creature, and put on its skin.

The spirit power of the monster was transferred to him and he was able to swim like a fish. Then a famine struck his home village and, binding his wife to secrecy, he put on his magic skin, caught some large fish, and left them by his mother-in-law's house. When she arose the next morning, she told all the people she herself had caught the fish because she was a shaman. She was a fraud, but the people honored her. The man and his wife laughed secretly. Then one morning when the young man did not return from fishing, his wife heard all the Ravens calling. She knew this was a sign that her husband was dead, for the spirits had told him he must return before the Raven people awakened. On the beach were two whales. (In some versions it is unclear whether the man's village was on the lake or on the ocean front. If the former is the case, then up in Tlingit land is a noteworthy parallel to the legends of the "inland whales" of the California Indians.)

The grieving wife found a "monster" lying on the beach between the two whales. Investigating further, the people found the missing young husband dead inside the monster's skin. The secret was now out; the widow told all. Now the people knew who had brought fish to their village to alleviate the famine, and they knew also that the dead man was a true hero with spirit power. Because he had been overloaded with the two whales, he had been unable to get home before "the Ravens called." They had a great funeral and placed his bones in a grave box in a tree "near the lake back of the village." Thereafter he was spoken of as the "Gunah-kah-daht."

One night while mourning at her husband's

grave, the young widow heard him call to her: "Climb on my back." So together they went to the supernatural home of the Gunah-kah-daht and for this reason it is good fortune when anyone sees this being and his descendants who are at the headwaters of many streams. In Haida mythology this being becomes the Sea Wolf or Wasgo.

In others of the infinite versions, this being saves the young man's brother-in-law, and discloses the mother-in-law's fraudulent claim to be a shaman so that she dies of her shame.

Toward the south of the totem region Thunderbird is the great protector of fishermen, and the supernatural Killer Whale does *not* aid the Indian. The winter ceremonies al-

ways featured spirit dancers showing how their ancestors fought the enemy of all Indians.

Who has not heard of the Abominable Snowman of the Himalaya Mountains on the northern frontier of India?

We have them—or so it is said—on the Northwest Coast even today. Called in the vernacular either Bigfoot or various Indian names interpreted generally as Timber Giant, these subhuman, hair-covered creatures are said to stand from seven to nine feet tall, the latter being the males. Weighing upward of five hundred pounds, they are said to roam the remaining vast forest lands from Northern California to well north of Juneau.

Cowichan Indians, of a large Coast Salish division, still hold occasional winter dances at which ancient myths are dramatically acted out. Here they portray a struggle with Killer Whale during a canoe voyage. (British Columbia Government)

The myth of the Cannibal Giants lives on in the modern Timber Giant, the Sasquatch of the Northwest Coast from Mendocino County, California, to southeast Alaska. Much evidence links these subhuman, upright-walking forest giants to the Abominable Snowman of India, Nepal, and Tibet. In the Fraser River valley. photographs were taken of footprints. This one, typical, measures some fourteen inches long and ten inches wide. (Photograph by Hal Rhodes)

But present-day Indians, educated ones of the ancient eight nations of Totemland, say, "The white man is hundreds of years late catching on to the idea of Sasquatch and Dsonoqua." It's a rare month that passes in the Pacific Northwest without a newspaper account of sightings and groups of whites and Indians mounting a search. Yes, the author has engaged in some on-the-spot research regarding this myth creature that is a living legend to thousands and an affidavit sworn reality to others.

Supernatural? Of course not. Do these creatures really exist? Quite possibly. Listen. . . .

For years the giant cannibal Goo-teekhl had ravaged the Tlingit villages of the Chilkat people, according to recorded accounts given by the natives about 1890. Arrows and spears would not kill them. Finally the warriors of

the Frog clan made a pitfall and by a ruse one of the giants was trapped. Then the creature was bound with ropes and nets made of sinew. A fire was built and the creature—no one would say he was supernatural—was put on the fire. For several days eulachon oil and wood were added until the creature was consumed. But the winds scattered the ashes and from them arose swarms of mosquitoes. Here a fairly reasonable legend, or tradition, seems to go mythical in a northland saga reminiscent of the Phoenix bird of the Old World.

The Tlingit said that Goo-teekhl's thirst for blood was transmitted to mosquitoes in a supernatural manner. (Anyone who has rambled around over Alaska and the Yukon will agree that the mosquitoes are very large and their thirst for human blood unquenchable.) The myth part has it that "good luck follows those

The mythical Cannibal Giant (masked and gesturing figure carrying Whale totem in right hand) rushes on stage to attack Indians in a ceremonial dance. This event, which is open to the public, is staged annually by the Chilkat-Tlingit dancers, in authentic costumes (Chilkat dance aprons and leggings with mukluk-type footwear), at the new Indian Community House at Haines-Port Chilkoot in Alaska. (Alaska Travel Division)

The terror of the waters, according to the mythology of the southernmost Tlingit of the Cape Fox, Alaska, area, was Giant Clam. Sometimes also called Rock Oyster, this creature devoured canoes. On the bottom of this pole, which now stands at Saxman, Alaska, is Clam with his teeth clenched on the arm of a man who was drowned by the rising tide. (Alaska Travel Division)

who dream of Goo-teekhl." For many years, until recently, some of these cannibal figures were given a daily "meal" of oil. Consequently several such figures are known to exist in the houses of old native families in southeastern Alaska. Precisely where is seldom known because, though the tradition persists, the totem owners are understandably reticent about showing their family house posts to strangers who rarely understand the ancient lore.

Of all the odd supernaturals, Giant Clam, Rock Oyster, and a huge Crab would seem the most out of place. We know the first of these creatures does exist in the warm waters of the South Seas, but Northwest Coast waters are cold. Yet the Koryak of Siberia have myths of the monstrous crabs and, accepting the generally held view of prehistoric migrations of Mongol races from Asia across the Bering Sea, there is a possible legendary link. The Totemland aborigines almost certainly met Kanaka seamen from Polynesia in late prehistoric or early historic times and the tradition could have started at such a meeting. Embellishments incident to retellings are to be expected.

Thus the supernatural Crab, so large no other living creature of sea or land could prevail against him, caught on with the Naden River Haida of the Queen Charlotte Islands. A legendary Chief Rock had such a Crab servant. His waterfront was never assaulted by any foe until a boy with Halibut's skin overcame it by spirit power after swimming around the world. Jules Verne was a piker compared to these mythmakers.

As for the supernatural bivalves, the Tlingit of Cape Fox, Alaska, and the Tsimsyan of nearby Port Simpson, B.C., have long had this tradition. Curiously, relatively few poles employed this fearsome being of the deep either as part of a story or as a crest. The most famous existing clam pole (in Saxman, Alaska) depicts Clam with his ferocious teeth clenching a man's arm.

Serpent, the harbinger of evil, is still all over the southern half of the totem area and in many varieties, some with two heads. A maker

The preserved remains of an old totem pole on the Quinault reservation (Coast Salish tribe) are overlooked by most researchers. Of substantial interest are the totems being held by the human figure. The figures (from top down) are: a water bird; Salmon; Hai-et-lik, the mythical supernatural serpent of Nootka lore; and Seal or Sea Lion.

of lightning and able to shed its scales when attacked, the Hai-et-lik of the Nootka has only one head. On the Olympic Peninsula this creature once was on many poles. The Quinault (a Salish tribe) and the independent Quilliute probably obtained the myth from the Makah-Nootka at Cape Flattery. Great whalers, the Nootka believed the scales of the great snake gave them supernatural power in the hunt for the leviathans of the deep.

The Sisiutl, the two-headed serpent of the Kwakiutl, was a supernatural creature said, in the lore of the British Columbia coast and Vancouver Island, to be four feet in diameter and up to twenty feet long. At times it was in league with Thunderbird and made thunder and lightning. Its "house" was either on land or in water. The body had an identical head at each end, with a human face, implying soul power, midway between. Almost always caus-

ing death when encountered, it was all the more dangerous because it could shrink itself to a tiny fraction of its true length.

Another two-headed serpent, Tsi-a-kish, was so large it swallowed canoes. One myth tells how a folk hero encountered one so large that when he sang a certain song, it burst open and an entire tribe came forth in something of a multiple Jonah release.

As the cultural level of the Indians increased, the mythology took on the aspects of heraldry in the same evolutionary way that the epic period of Anglo-Saxon history developed. Thus many of the frightful monsters and the supernatural beings with delegated powers of creation became valued guardian spirits displayed as crests on totem poles. The myths lived on but the powers of their spirits became the tools of the shaman and the badges of rank, as it were, of the nobility.

Carved by Kwakiutl Chief Nakapenkim (Mungo Martin) in 1940, this archway to Thunderbird Park in Victoria, British Columbia, shows the two-headed monster Sisiutl in a manner once popular among the Kwakiutls. Such a carving often formed the front horizontal house beam. Thunderbird sits on top of Serpent.

Guardian-spirit Powers
and Crest Symbols

Superstition, common among aboriginal cultures, combined with an abstract religious concept, was destined to produce a vast mythology. The developmental stages of mystical devotion to the transformable supernatural beings might have been reversed. The fairly complex spiritual growth unfolded during the scores of centuries prior to the European explorations. The evolution of the native philosophy on the North Pacific Coast cannot be firmly established because of its isolation and a complete absence of any written language.

The Chinook jargon, a late prehistoric synthesis of very limited vocabulary, was the principal vehicle by which the picturesquely thoughtful creation stories of the northern nations filtered into the southern part of the region. The latter's mythology was largely adapted from that of the northerners who were the most artfully skilled and widely traveled. Consequently the myths already examined are, in the main, of northern origination.

Conversely the intricacies of the guardian-spirit tradition were more pronounced among the Kwakiutl, Bella Coola, Coast Salish, and Nootka than among their northern neighbors. As the social system expanded regionally, however, the very human urge to excel, and thus gain possessions and prestige, required a means to communicate personal attainment. The crest system—much like the heraldry of Europe—solved the problem. Having a relatively fine dwelling was a start, but an understandable picture signpost, that any equally unlettered friend or foe could interpret, solved all problems save one: what to put on the crest.

Lineage was only one aspect of the regional totemism, but when blended with personal mysticism, the custom flowered and by the turn of the century—when it withered—there were more than a hundred distinct guardian

This very old Gitksan-Tsimsyan pole in the Indian village at Kispiox, British Columbia, shows Beaver (above man) in an unusual representation —his scaly tail is hanging downward, and he lacks the almost invariably shown long upper front teeth. (British Columbia Government)

Quite unusual, this is the Loon Tree Totem, now preserved in the Saxman, Alaska, park. Loon is at the top, followed by three Bear cubs. At the bottom is Bear Mother, a crest of the Tlingit "Kats House" people. (Pacific Northern Airlines)

It is reliably reported by Northwest Coast anthropologists who have treated with the Kitwancool that this tribe erected totems one thousand years ago. This is a portion of a badly decayed pole that has been taken to Victoria for restoration under terms of agreement with the owners, the Frog clan of the Kitwancool, whose origins in tribal records trace back to the Biblical flood.

spirits. The benefits showered on a protégé overlapped in many instances, but there were specific boons available from each. The symbols portraying the various spirits gradually became somewhat standardized—more so than were the genealogical and myth-figure symbols providing the history, or story line, on the totem poles.

Insofar as the author can ascertain, the following extensive list of guardian spirits is the first to appear in a popular book. Persons given to a leisurely study of Indian lore, and travelers to the region, are likely to find this compilation valuable and accurate. The design characteristics of each crest symbol, when such are reasonably standardized, will be included in each description. The guardian spirits are listed alphabetically, not in order of descending popularity, though Bear, the first one, happens to be one of the most common.

BEAR, either black or brown, is one of the most eagerly sought guardian spirits because of the beast's great strength and popularity as a mythical ancestor.

Women who gain this spirit become industrious and skilled as housekeepers, fine cooks, and good mothers. Men protégés become skilled hunters possessing great endurance.

Grizzly's spirit grants greater strength, allowing his protégés to perform feats of skill and daring, especially in spirit dances. Devotees, when not properly initiated by a shaman, often become uncontrollable and frenzied while dancing, and they are said to have short lives unless they cleanse themselves after such a seizure. Grizzly is usually shown with protruding tongue, but there are exceptions to this, of course.

BEAVER, called Tsing by the Haida, is usually shown with his scaly tail pointing upward and with a log or fish clutched in his forepaws. Almost always he can be identified easily by his very long incisor teeth.

This spirit bestows "medicine power" and ability to change snow or bitterly cold weather to rain or mist by chanting his song. During creation he was a large animal.

Around 1800, the symbol of beaver on a totem pole indicated that the owner was very wealthy (the fur trade with Europeans increased this spirit's attraction). He is still an important clan crest.

CORMORANT is a beneficial spirit to fishermen, imparting skill in spearing salmon particularly. When carved (and that in the North and seldom), he looks somewhat like Raven but has horizontal fluted marks below each eye.

COUGAR or MOUNTAIN LION confers "medicine power," but more often bestows greater than average skill in fishing, hunting, tracking, and stalking wild game, especially deer and rabbits. Though a powerful spirit and giver of songs, he is almost never seen as a crest.

DEER enables his protégé to approach deer with ease and to spear them at close range. The creatures will act as if they are the protégé's friends.

Though many spirits can be attained by a white person, Deer's is strictly reserved for Indians. This is the will of Raven and "He who dwells above."

DOG is a spirit who is particularly sought after by the Indians farther north. The Tlingit and Haida and upriver Tsimsyan-Niskae and Gitksan tribes consider Dog the most powerful of all. In dances his protégé becomes fierce and dangerous and can suffer evil. A shaman's assistance is often necessary to avoid death. His symbol is rare and not standardized, but if it appears on a totem pole it is usually realistic. Dog was the only domesticated animal on the Northwest Coast. Shamans frequently cast spells on a foe by calling on this spirit.

DOGFISH is a rarely obtained spirit. He who gains favor of Dogfish has great ability to learn and sing many songs and chants, and he is a skillful dancer. One poor soul who possessed this spirit is said to have been crippled

BEAVER

BEAR

DOGFISH

so badly from birth that he had to crawl about on his knees. Hence he had difficulty dancing, but he was a great singer and was loved because he had the power of song and gave of it freely.

Shown less frequently than many symbols, Dogfish is recognized by a high and rounded vaulted forehead and is often confused with Shark.

DUCK is very powerful, so much so that protégés frequently become possessed as when performing his dance. He imparts great skill in fishing but is no friend of the hunter, for he sometimes warns deer and bear of the approach of a hunter even if the latter is his supplicant. Duck is seldom carved, but his symbol is realistic, generally with half-spread wings.

EAGLE endows the favored person with skill as a hunter of all kinds of game both feathered and furred, with penetrating eyesight, and with exceptional hearing. Occasionally he warns of approaching enemies and, in the dance, enables one to fly about the room. His song is piercing and punctuated with screams and spine-tingling shrieks. A northern spirit and a family as well as clan crest, he favors those who live near mountains. In the southern nations his attributes are ascribed, generally, to Thunderbird. His beak always curves downward.

FLY always lurks in the vicinity of animals, so this spirit aids hunters if they have cleansed themselves properly, learned the songs, and have been fervent in the quest.

FROG was a companion supernatural of Raven "in the beginning." When revealing himself, he is invariably a huge bullfrog. A watchman, he warns of enemies by croaking deeply. One knows he has gained Frog's spirit when he hears Frog cry like a human baby. Frog brings people good fortune. So powerful is this spirit that it should *never* be portrayed in winter dances.

Portrayed quite realistically with a wide mouth and no teeth, Frog is a prime crest, proving an ancient and fruitful lineage.

One of the most ancient and interesting Frog stories, describing the origin of a clan and this spirit's symbol as a crest, is that of the noted Nee-Gamks pole of the Kitwancool made by Chief Ak-gwen-dasqu ("it is forbidden to touch him"). The story is long and of an ancient people led by Chief Gwen-nue, who, when the "flood" was foretold, built a raft for his entire tribe. When the waters subsided, the raft grounded near present Ketchikan, Alaska.

In search of a suitable site, the tribe finally came to a place called Git-ha-guns, where they established temporary homes.

The next spring the chief's sister disappeared. After a time two small frogs came to the chief's lodge and knew him as their grandfather and refused to leave. Wise men were summoned. The young frogs kept repeating "Ze-weed" and "Ga-dath." A wise woman was called in; she said the names were given the little frogs by their mother, the chief's sister, who had been taken by a nearby frog clan and was now married to the chief of the frogs.

EAGLE

The Kitwancool chief and his warriors drained the nearby lake. A flying frog came out and was stabbed by a warrior who took it for his crest. Soon the chief's sister, Nee-gamks, appeared riding on the back of her husband, the frog chief, and singing the funeral song "Lemk-ks-goax-qu Nee-gamks," which is sung ceremonially to this day and means "they floated out of the water." The song was then given to Nee-gamks' brother, the chief. Nee-gamks, having taken on the form of a frog and preferring to remain with the frog clan, bade her brother farewell. The tribe still exists and two clans are the Wolf and Frog, the latter directly descended, according to the ancient songs, from Chief Gwen-nue.

GOAT (specifically MOUNTAIN GOAT) makes the protégé fleet of foot, a good climber, and a fine hunter of mountain game. His spirit also invokes kindness, good humor, and fair play, but this must be bilateral, to use a modern term. Goat was sometimes portrayed on totems in erect standing position with front legs folded across his chest and smiling. He has long horns. A powerful spirit embraced, in first instance, by mountain Indians and later by those living near water. Related to Goat's spirit is one that "dwells far out to sea" and bestows fishing skill. This "sea" spirit has the form of a human with hair reaching to the elbows; he is dressed with red-dyed cedar bark in bands around his head, elbows, and waist.

HAWK as a guardian spirit was a rarity, but as a crest he was popular. By a sharply reverse-curved beak, his symbol is distinguished from that of Eagle. He was favored on mortuary poles, and legend has it that Haida chiefs feuded over the right to own Hawk crests.

HOHOQ or SKOKOK (Kwakiutl and Coast Salish, respectively) is a very special spirit bird of the mountains. Sometimes he looks like a white owl; at other times he has an extraordinary long beak. Those who own him as guardian spirit are particularly skilled as sturgeon fishermen. Seldom does he appear as a crest, but usually depicts an event of distinction and was quite common on house-front or portal poles.

HORNET spirit makes its home in the bitterly cold North and his protégé becomes a strong

GOAT

HAWK

warrior as well as a fine hunter and fisherman who can always gather his food easily and endure hardship during a difficult hunt or in war. The same attributes are Wasp's.

HUMMING BIRD, diminutive and swift, makes his protégé a fast runner and a good warrior with fine eyesight. Sometimes, reportedly, his protégé is granted medicine power and always skill with weapons.

KINGFISHER, "in the beginning," received the same words as Mink. In addition he grants navigational skills and protects those in dangerous waters.

LICE are never still but always moving. Because of this, the Lice spirit makes his protégé very industrious. The Lice of the Northwind also keep fish, mainly sturgeon, constantly on the move, so protégés acquire great fortune fishing for this creature.

LOON gives women great skill in weaving and sewing. Men with this spirit become fine fishermen. When shown on poles, Loon is usually at the top with wings in the diving position. Among the Tlingit, Loon once had status as a family or personal crest.

MAGPIE, the sharp-eyed guard of the land, is a spirit of good fortune in every honorable endeavor. Magpie, a friend of Raven, also gives acutely good eyesight to the faithful, but the author can find no record of a pole showing this bird.

MINK was another of Raven's companions when the world was dark. In fact, Raven at times borrowed this creature's skin. The more southern Indians believed the Creator told Mink that he would confer power on recipients to "catch fish easily by night or day." There is believed to be a relationship between Mink and Kingfisher, and Mink is also a helper and protector of Salmon. Mink is an "arranger"; his protégés call upon him whenever there is domestic strife or difficulties of a personal nature with other Indians.

MOLE (specifically the shale mole) is rarely shown on poles. His protégés are women and they acquire special skill in all aspects of woman's work.

MOSQUITO is another busy spirit and, despite his appetite for blood, is symbolic of the soul's immortality. To shamans, Mosquito imparts ability to heal the sick if the protégé has faithfully purified himself and fasted. If he has not done so, he cannot cure, but he will cause illness to afflict others.

OWL, the white owl or snow bird, gives skill and strength as a fisher of sturgeon primarily, but also of halibut and salmon. (His cousin, GREAT HORNED OWL, is a guardian spirit of medicine men.) He also helps ordinary people (after proper fasting and cleansing, and singing, of course) to become excellent hunters on sea and land for all game in foul and fair weather. Only rarely does Owl appear on poles as a crest.

RACCOON will make a man rich if the endowed person is humble, and he lets his protégés work safely with fire because Coon cannot be smoked out of a tree. The Coast Salish believe Coon is responsible for nightmares and wild dreams. He was not popular as a crest.

RAVEN was the most popular crest figure in the north. In the south he was valued as a guardian spirit but less often seen on poles.

Possessors of this spirit are fine hunters who enjoy special ease in killing game. Raven's immortal spirit also cleans up remains of animals, and the trash careless people leave about. Raven enjoys a clean landscape; he was the great "arranger." Protégés must be clean in their daily lives.

His symbol has a short, straight beak and, in the north, he often appears holding the light box and with a circle, representing Sun, around his head.

SALMON, the symbol of fertility, immortality, and wealth for all Indians, conferred special incantation powers on devotees whose quest in youth established him as guardian spirit. Protégés could also influence the weather, prevent or change excessive cold snaps, and change snow to rain. Oddly, this principal food fish's spirit was rarely carved as a totem crest.

SANDHILL CRANE's spirit is related to that of Mole. Most of Sandhill Crane's protégés were women; they became especially skilled in female tasks such as spinning wool, making clothing, skinning animals, and drying and smoking salmon for the winter's food supply. Mainly a southern-area spirit, Crane was almost never seen on poles but was sometimes etched on wooden boxes and other artifacts.

SCULPIN or BULLHEAD, a chunky, tough trash fish and very ugly, was often used as a design on dishes and the like. Few poles carried his visage or representation, but on his rare appearances he was carved with two hornlike protrusions over the mouth and (when shown full length) a head-to-tail dorsal fin. His spirit attributes are unknown. The Gitrhahla, a Tsimsyan tribe, took Giant Sculpin, a landlocked "flood" victim, as its crest.

SEA GULL was primarily a spirit highly regarded by the Nootka. His favor was in a protective capacity. When seen on poles, and this was seldom, he was usually at the top. Sea gull sometimes rescued stranded fishermen and was said to have flown some to the safety of land.

SEAL (or SEA LION) was quite popular as a crest in Bella Coola country; less so elsewhere. He was only rarely held as a guardian spirit but he did give swimming and fishing skill. He was a symbol of wealth.

SEA OTTER makes recipients skilled hunters of seals or sea lions, and to a lesser degree, good fishermen. Most important was that those who had his blessing were destined to wealth.

SERPENT and several dragonlike beings never achieved true guardian-spirit stature. They were primarily fearsome creatures.

SHARK was, in the main, a spirit to be feared. Medicine men claimed his power at times. His symbol is similar to that of Dogfish, but it has a lower, flatter forehead. At each side of his toothy mouth, there were several curved gill marks.

RAVEN

SHARK

SKUNK, who has to be besieged with many incantations, fasting, and cleansing, imparts healing power to medicine men. There is no established crest symbol. Shamans, in the south, appear to be the principal protégés.

SNAIL seems to have been a spirit similar to Woodgrub. His crest is confused and controversial. Research fails to define his benefits or whether he was, in fact, a guardian spirit.

SNAKE (the common nonpoisonous coastal garter snake) was a tutelary spirit that granted magic powers. Some protégés were said to suspend ropes between opposite walls without tying either end. This mysterious power, similar to that of East Indian sorcerers, is said to exist today in isolated Indian villages.

STURGEON is a rare guardian spirit, but Indians who are careful to purify themselves continuously before maturity might obtain this great fish spirit that enables a protégé to know exactly where to fish for great numbers of sturgeon, and exactly how to catch or spear them. As a crest it has no established symbol.

TIMBER GIANTS, CANNIBAL GIANTS, and such creatures are said to convey power on rare occasions to one who purifies himself daily and is then the only person who can ever meet this creature-spirit of the forest. Once the spirit is won, the bearer can perform great feats of strength such as shaking the trunk of a huge tree so that all of its bark falls off.

Indians say, "Only Indian can meet Sasquatch. Sasquatch not like white man 'cause he smell bad."

THUNDERBIRD, as a guardian spirit evolved from a parallel concept with Raven of ancient mythology, is known throughout Siberia and half of North America. Regionalized on the North Pacific Coast, he is, to the Coast Salish, chief of all guardian spirits by order and creation of Khaals. He has many characteristics of the eagle; he sometimes resembles certain hawks; and he occasionally looks like some

large water birds. Tatooch, or Tsoona, is the instrument of "He who dwells above" and carries out the creative will, including creating other spirits, the elements, and so forth. When he flies, his flapping wings cause thunder and his flashing eyes cause lightning. As a totem crest the position of the wings conveys the crest owner's feeling as to Thunderbird power in his life.

Living in the highest mountains, he eats Killer Whales and sometimes sharks and rays. The protector of good Indians, he is, to southern tribes, the most important of all spirits. Among other tribes, he is the giant Sparrow Hawk, Skyai-msen or Scam-sum.

TROUT is such a powerful spirit, it is restricted to medicine men except on Vancouver Island where mystics of lower rank occasionally are so endowed. A great healing spirit, Trout enables the purified medicine man to draw out sicknesses, even tumors, from the body by both physical and spiritual means.

WARRIOR SPIRIT is a dual being: one is joyful, the other is powerful and gives the recipient good luck in all he does. The Indian so endowed can make blood ooze from his mouth, painlessly, while dancing. Not of animal origin, there is no totem symbol.

WATER BIRD exists as a spirit in several aquatic species, including the murre, and has the power to discover floating things on the sea. After such a discovery Water Bird calls other birds to the feast. This spirit gives the power to gain worldly goods, so that the protégé can give many potlatches and fine gifts. Bering Sea Eskimos and the Tlingit and Haida call the murre the "Old Man" because of its appearance; it resembles and nests like a penguin. The murre migrates, to this day, as far south as northern California in winter. This spirit bestows good sight and ability to garner great wealth. Tourists frequently think of the totem symbol as a penguin. A regional legend is "the murres spend much time painting their eggs."

W H A L E

W O L F

WHALE is especially feared as he often tips over dugouts of hunting parties—a bad spirit that makes one destructive. BLACKFISH, though smaller, is related. Most inhabitants of the seas flee at approach of Blackfish as this spirit is tremendously powerful. One so endowed becomes a skilled hunter of seals and water birds and a good fisherman for salmon and halibut.

WOLF bestows its happy spirit to help people. Coast Salish search for this spirit in order to become fine hunters. Women obtaining this spirit become skilled weavers and blanket and mat makers. The holders of Wolf's spirit also become skilled in woodcraft, and their senses are extraordinarily highly developed. As a crest symbol Wolf frequently clutches his sectioned tail with forepaws, has prominent nostrils, and occasionally a nose that is quite long.

The elements and cosmic bodies are powerful spirits in their own right. According to the Indian myth complex, each was, ages ago, supernatural, with both human and divine forms:

AURORA BOREALIS (Northern Lights) were believed by the farthest north tribes to be torches in the hands of spirits seeking souls of those who are about to die. These spirits, when desiring to speak with living people, make whistling sounds and one must answer promptly but in whispers.

SOUTH WIND enables a man to run over the surface of the water.

WEST WIND gives power to become a great warrior whose prayers càn prevent storms from striking.

THUNDER, a winter-dance spirit, requires the protégé to paint his face black like a thundercloud before doing the specified dance. Then, if properly purified, he can cause thunder to clap loudly by raising his hand to the sky and sometimes cause lightning to strike causing fire. Some women are so endowed. This is pure sorcery and mesmerizes both dancer and audience.

STAR protégés are able to find the "lost vitalities" or souls of ailing Indians because stars survey the entire world. This, then, is a Medicine Spirit to be invoked to heal the sick of body and mind.

SUN, source of life and suspended in the sky because Raven put it there, is the spirit of the center of the solar system and gives recipients songs and chants to use when engaged in warfare; makes them strong and brave warriors. A protégé, however, must be just and fair or he will lose his power, be shamed, and die. As a totem symbol Sun is generally shown with Raven, and the stories told of them are the Indian's genesis.

As crests, the guardian-spirit symbols became the personal identifications of the chiefs who owned the totem poles. In a sense a crest was a chief's personal banner: it was carved on his halibut club, his canoe paddle, on his grease box, and on his cedar-slat armor. Many Indians owned several crests, requiring exceptionally complex poles of various types, as different in their own way as was the crest complex.

7

Totem Poles— and the Stories They Tell

We have spoken of the rise of totemism and its application to the indigenous art forms of the area which, until comparatively recently, was the most generally isolated as regards outside contact by the native inhabitants in comparison with those of the great plains and the Rocky Mountain region.

But to understand clearly the significance of totem poles in the lusty native culture, we must examine the several distinctive types. To consider these poles merely awe-inspiring, as some casual visitors have observed, is to ignore their true historic value. They *are* awe-inspiring, but that is only part of their attraction for us. One cannot stroll casually through a collection of restored and preserved totem poles without becoming curious about the meanings of the many figures.

If any single class of object is universally representative of the native arts of this vast region—known generally as the Pacific Northwest—it must be the "tall totem pole," the distinctive manifestation of a culture almost as extinct as it was once extensive and unbelievably vigorous.

A discussion of totem-pole types requires, first, a correction of the common misconception of their purpose in the prehistoric and in the early centuries of the historical period of this continent. As already mentioned, these poles, or the symbolical figures on them, were *not* worshiped; they were never voodoolike in use or intent.

What, then, is a *totem pole?*

Dictionary answers synthesize into something like this: a pole, post, or pillar carved and painted by hand with symbols or figures of a totemic nature and placed in front of the dwellings of several "Indian tribes of the Northwest Coast of North America."

Only vaguely satisfactory, this definition presupposes an understanding of "totemism."

Specifically, we must remember that the symbols on totem poles were the aboriginal substitutes for the printed word. The totem pole was the signboard, the genealogical record, the memorial, and the classified advertisement of the region. It was the publicity campaign of the man of distinction and, through personal crests, identified him and his family, his clan, and occasionally his tribe, and told of important events in the factual and mythological past.

This brings us to the six principal types of totem poles and to the conclusion, despite much learned controversy to the contrary, that they all fulfill the dictionary definition of such poles. We shall examine some varieties that are generally little-known but were more numerous than the familiar and obvious "tall totem pole" of travel-folder fame.

Actually the most numerous totem figures were *not* on "tall poles" at all.

The six principal totem-pole types are (1) memorial or heraldic poles, (2) grave figures, (3) house posts, (4) house-front or portal poles, (5) welcoming or waterfront-owner poles, and (6) mortuary poles. Considering the Pacific Northwest as a whole, the types named are listed in their over-all order of importance. The number of each type or total number of all types that proudly stood at any one time during what Indians call "the old days" will probably never be known.

There is one other category—an important, exciting, sensational, and rare type that is remarkable because the samples were often one of a kind. These were the ridicule and shame

Of comparatively recent origin is this Haida memorial pole carved about 1925 by one of the few active native carvers of the time, Robert Ridley of Masset in the Queen Charlotte Islands. Now standing in Thunderbird Park in Victoria, British Columbia, this totem is less boldly executed than the ancient poles. The symbols (from top down) are: Eagle with wings folded, meaning peace, holding small face figure meaning the soul; Indian medicine man wearing headdress and holding a medicine or soul-catching device in each hand; Beaver (without usual horizontal stick in forepaws) with soul symbol between hind legs; Bear Mother with cub child; Frog with head down; and Eagle.

This well-preserved but much too garishly painted pole, which now stands in Wenatchee, Washington, is a fine Kwakiutl memorial totem from Alert Bay, British Columbia. Symbols (from top down) are: Thunderbird with widely spread wings, showing vigorous life; Grizzly Bear or Bear Mother with forepaws over small head (indicating either a child or the pole owner who owns Bear crest or is a protégé of Bear guardian spirits, or symbolizing inner spirit or soul); the trapezoid-shaped shield device with stylized facial features represents a valued copper to emphasize wealth and influence of pole owner; Shale Mole (with upcurved tail) is a woman's guardian spirit and no doubt honors chief's wife; the large figure at the bottom is not definitely identified but the poorly executed Frog being held probably indicates Frog clan relationship.

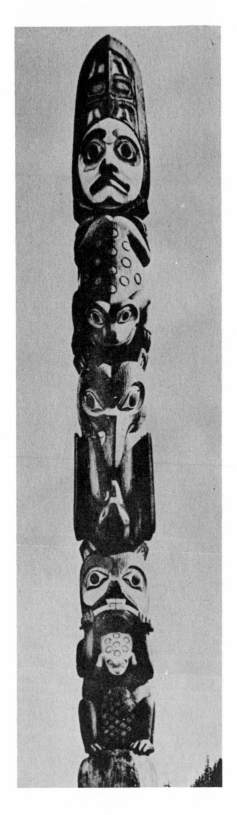

poles, almost exclusively Haida and Tlingit creations, devised for specific, sudden, and sometimes scandalous, reasons.

Caution is advised: we are not attempting to *read* any of these poles.[1] Totem poles cannot be read in the accepted sense of the word, but, with a knowledge of the symbols, the mythology, and the historic facts of the clans and tribes concerned, as well as of the social customs and traditions of the original inhabitants, they can be interpreted.

Every part of each figure has a definite meaning, and the combinations on each pole, post, or pillar relate either a myth, a folk legend with a basis in fact, a definitely established historic fact or event in the life of the pole owner or of the ancestral lineage of his family or, less frequently, of his tribe. Occasionally his wife's lineage is memorialized, especially by the three Haida divisions. Crests are usually displayed, and guardian-spirit symbols are prominently shown.

In a sense, and according to Indian custom, every totem pole is memorial in essence, though it may not necessarily fall into that classification or be designed for that function.

Of all the structures and artifacts of Totemland, none was more highly regarded than the memorial pole. Back "in the old days" before

[1] A national magazine, in publishing a totem-pole feature by this author, made a common error (and disregarded the author's caution) by titling the feature "How to Read Totem Poles."

Called the Kahl-teen totem by the Kiksadi (a Tlingit clan of Raven phratry, once living around present-day Sitka and Wrangell), this memorial pole was erected about 1900 in memory of a high chief, called Kilteen by the whites, and is now under the protection of the U.S. Forest Service. This pole shows (from top down): the little-known spirit Person-of-the-Glacier; Frog; a Raven child between vertically positioned wings—a uniquely rendered Raven clan crest of the Kiksadi; Beaver as a principal guardian-spirit symbol with a small Frog above Beaver's universally scaly tail. (Winter & Pond)

the invading European culture became widespread, the chief of every clan house would erect a memorial pole to honor the deceased chief and to confirm his own lineage and the rights and prerogatives accruing to him under the customary hereditary succession. Tsimsyan poles of this type tended to be the highest in all Totemland, often more than fifty feet tall. Among the Niskae tribes, some poles, called *kan,* are said to have approached eighty feet and usually had carvings only at top and bottom, the intervening wood being smooth. Poles with carvings the full length were not as tall but tended to be much thicker; called *ptsaen,* they were split down the center and hollowed. The Haida generally carved poles full length, calling solid poles *rhat* and hollowed semicircular poles *gyalken.* Hollowing tall poles was common practice as it minimized splitting and increased the pole's life.

Sometimes erroneously called "potlatch pole" (since it was the type usually erected at such an event), the memorial pole was essentially heraldic in nature, with personal and lineage crest symbols predominating. Guardian-spirit symbols were also used on these poles. Among the southern Tlingit tribes there was a tendency to honor the wife's lineage, with her totem symbol at the extreme top. Kwakiutl tribes also followed this custom, but, in some instances, placed the wife's symbols lower.

Possibly one hundred years of age or more is this Kwakiutl pole, which was collected in 1914 from Tsawadi village on Knight Inlet, British Columbia. It had stood there for "many decades" say officials of Thunderbird Park in Victoria, British Columbia, where it now stands beautifully preserved. Symbols (from top down) are: Thunderbird, with life-indicating outspread wings; the legendary Dsonoqua, the wild Cannibal Giant of the deep forests, also called Sasquatch by many northwest tribes (the Northwest Coast equivalent of the famed Abominable Snowman of the India-Tibet borderlands); and two chiefs displaying valuable coppers often worth several thousand blankets in the native economy. Such figures as the latter are somewhat unusual on memorial poles.

In essence, memorial poles combined symbols honoring a recently deceased chief with symbols confirming the line of succession. These were the finest, most revered of all poles. Unfortunately, comparatively few of them remain well preserved as their great height and weight render collection and transport difficult.

The Kwakiutl, Bella Coola, Nootka, and Coast Salish to the south also erected such poles, but they tended to be lower, forty feet or less.

Grave figures, which were more numerous than any other type, were erected with less consideration for rank if sufficient payment goods could be collected from survivors. Grave figures were usually of animal, bird, or sea creatures—the personal totem of the deceased. An enormous figure of this type impressed the Spanish explorer Malaspina in 1792 at Yaku-

tat, seat of the Huna tribe of the Tlingit. Grave shelters were also common; shed-shaped and small, these structures often enclosed a grave box beneath a cedar bark roof with the grave figure close beside, and were invariably used for interment of Tlingit *iktuhs*.

Among the Tlingit and Haida, horizontal figures are common, but not exclusively so, and they are often in combination with a supplementary symbol.

The Tsimsyan, Kwakiutl, Bella Coola, and Coast Salish tribes favored upright animal figures but also employed occasional human figures. Among the more northern Indians, the ancient practice was to entomb the deceased's remains in a carved box that, in the case of vertical markers, was often placed on top of the grave figure. Although most of these Indians have converted, at least nominally, to Christianity, this totem-figure custom is not

The restoration of this old Quilliute Thunderbird grave figure was enhanced by replacing the decayed wings with new, but unauthentic, sawmill boards. While the shining white paint preserves, it is not the color usually favored by the Indians of old. (Not shown in the illustration is Whale at the feet of Thunderbird.)

LEFT: *The Bella Coola carved some of the finest and most interesting of the once-numerous grave totems. The decayed original of this exact replica, which duplicates even the native adz markings, was collected from Talio, the principal village of the Bella Coola, in 1913. Grizzly Bear was the principal guardian spirit of the dead chief and Beaver was either a secondary guardian spirit, a personal crest, or was included to honor the deceased's surviving widow.* RIGHT: *Grizzly Bear was a favorite grave figure of the Bella Coola because he was a supernatural spirit always present in "the house of the Cannibal spirit." The original stood in Talio until about 1913, when, in decaying condition, it was removed with the owners' consent. Duplicated exactly by native carvers, this totem is now in Thunderbird Park in Victoria, British Columbia. In the palms of the forepaws are eyes that reflect either of two aboriginal concepts: the indication of the human-form wrist joints, or the symbol of the eternal life and sight of "the inner spirit" or soul of the deceased.*

In a place of honor by the entrance to the Totem Bight Park near Ketchikan, Alaska, is this restored Eagle grave figure. An unusual feature of the pole is the horizontally fluted treatment of the ears which is more characteristic of southern tribes. Whether Eagle has ears depends upon the style favored by the clan or tribe or the features of the crest symbol design of the pole owner. (Some of the forehead bird masks of the Kwakiutl and Nootka have exceptionally large ears with design work almost identical to that of the northern birds.) Legs, too, were treated variously on Eagle poles; the Haida and their Tlingit neighbors included legs on their Eagle figures more frequently than did the southern Totemland Indians. Kaigani-Haida and southern Tlingit art styles have long been related closely, and research cannot always disclose which "nation" created an isolated artifact. It is even possible that a southern carver could have been summoned north to carve this Eagle pole. More likely, however, it was made by a Haida or Tlingit carver who learned of this technique during a trade journey or war raid into Nootka or Kwakiutl country. (Alaska Travel Division)

In this restoration of an old Haida figure, the symbolic attack of Thunderbird on the evil Whale was intended to protect the owner and his seagoing canoe crew from injury and death. Such horizontal totems were once popular, but they are rare enough now to be considered as quite unusual. This is probably a memorial pole, although it is claimed as a grave figure by some Totemland authorities.

entirely dead. Many graveyards in Totemland have modern cement and stone totem markers.

House posts and pillars are believed to have been the most ancient of the totem-pole types; house posts were at least as numerous as grave figures and may even have been more prevalent. The universal custom was to decorate house interiors with as many house posts as wealth and space permitted. These posts combined the functional support of house beams with a handy surface on which crests, totems, and guardian-spirit symbols were carved. Only the Coast Salish appear to have carved

exterior posts along the sides of the house; these helped support roof structures.

The many symbols of supernatural beings that have been preserved on interior house posts provide an area of research for the continuing quest for Sasquatch, the legendary Timber Giant still frequently reported in western Washington, British Columbia, and as far south as mid-California. Salish, Nootka, and Quilliute (the small, completely independent "nation" with its own distinctive language and isolated islands at La Push, Washington) practice was to carve realistic animals proceeding down the pole in parade manner.

These two Coast Salish exterior house posts, which are estimated by archaeologist Albert B. Elsassar to be at least seventy years old, are considered reasonably good examples of pure Coast Salish poles. Except for the dance mask, an artifact at which they excelled, the Coast Salish were the least skilled in the plastic arts among the Totemland Indians. The posts now stand before the Robert H. Lowie Museum of Anthropology, University of California, Berkeley.

OPPOSITE: House-post totems were extensively used by all Totemland "nations" and are believed to be the earliest phase in the art of totem-pole carving. This exterior post, by an unidentified Koskimo-Kwakiutl, once supported the main beam in a chief's house on the shore of Quatsino Sound on Vancouver Island, British Columbia. (The steel rod at the middle of the pole is an effective way of supporting such restorations.) At the top is the powerful mythical Hohoq bird, which was a personal crest acquired through marriage by the chief who owned the house post. The human likeness below Hohoq represents one of a host of supernatural semimonsters who lived in the sea and had a culture combining attributes of humans, sea mammals, and spirits. At bottom is guardian spirit Grizzly Bear with a valued copper in his mouth, holding Whale whom, according to a tribal saga, he vanquished. This pole now stands in Thunderbird Park, Victoria, British Columbia.

This Quilliute house post represents one of the few remaining and preserved totem poles of this small "nation." The figures (from top down) are: a rarely seen symbol that seems to be Sea Gull; Serpent; an unidentified being that is probably the attempt of a carver with little skill to depict either Shark or Dogfish; and a bird creature with a hole between its eyes suggesting a one-time beak.

RIGHT: The Quinault tribe of the Olympic Peninsula claims these preserved remains of a Coast Salish house post. Extraordinarily rare on any pole is Murrellet at the top as he appears here. Bear, climbing, reverses the usual downward direction on Salish poles. The head-down position of Shark does not reflect the customary ridicule or shame because this type of pole is not common to the region. This pole is now at the U.S. Forestry station at Lake Quinault.

OPPOSITE: Twenty miles up the Chilkat River in [Kl]uk-wan, principal town of the Chilkat tribe of the [Tl]ingit, stood the great house of the Frog clan. As [wa]s the social custom, this was home-away-from-[ho]me for any peaceful traveling clan member with[ou]t regard to his tribal affiliations. Wondrous totems [fill]ed the noble vastness. The two in this photograph [by] the pioneer photographers Winter and Pond are [po]ssibly the most famed of all house posts in Totem[lan]d. The Frog clan pole stands behind the little clan [pr]incess; at her right is the figure of Goo-Teekhl, the [dr]ead Cannibal Giant who often terrorized Chilkat [vil]lages, stole children, and was impervious to spears [an]d arrows. (Winter & Pond)

The Kwakiutl often displayed crests of both sides of the family on these posts as did the Haida. The Tlingit had one particularly intriguing custom: one's status increased if one could secretly mutilate a prized interior post by carving away a portion of a symbol. All groups used movable posts which were not a part of the structural support. Many of the finest interior posts are still prized possessions of Indian families with ancient lineages.

The house-front or portal pole combined functions by acting both as a status symbol (by displaying inherited lineage and acquired crests) and as the only entrance to the house. These poles were from about twenty-five feet tall in the southern area to fifty feet among the Haida and Tsimsyan. Called *kerhen* by the Haida—whose entry portals were oval and seldom more than three feet in height—such poles were three to five feet wide at the base.

House-front or portal poles were less common among the Tlingit than among their Haida and Tsimsyan neighbors. However, this excellent example of a Tlingit portal pole was carved more than one hundred years ago on Village Island; now it is preserved in Saxman near Ketchikan. The symbolic figures represent the Kats family version of the Bear Mother "ancestor myth" quite common throughout Totemland's northern reaches. In this specific instance—only one of several versions among the Kagwantan-Tlingit who belonged to the Wolf phratry—the top figure represents Grizzly Bear woman who became the wife of Kats. The human face is that of Kats himself and he holds a small figure representing a descendant, one of two small orphans rejected by relatives because their faces were half bear and half human. Below Kats just above the house portal or doorway is a face representing Kats' grandmother. In some versions of this Kats family story, the grandmother was a princess who married Grizzly Bear. When her brothers came searching for her, they killed her Bear husband even though he had assumed the form of a human. In this latter version, a descendant of Kats married a Grizzly Bear woman. The Grizzly Bear crest signifies the Kagwantan are strong and influential. (Alaska Travel Division).

One of the most intricately carved poles, and a most unusual one in many respects, is this housefront totem from the old Bella Coola village of Talio, from which it was collected in 1913. It is curiously notched at the top—a feature not common to this type, for which no explanation exists. Below the notch is a distinctively Bella Coola etching of Beaver's face, lacking the almost universal crosshatched tail or teeth, while to each side are Raven symbols with flapping wings. The huge eyes belong to Hohoq, whose two-piece beak, fifteen feet long, was once supported by two squarish holes. Above the entry portal—where one must stoop—is a Seal family. The drawing shows how Hohoq's long bill looked when the pole was intact.

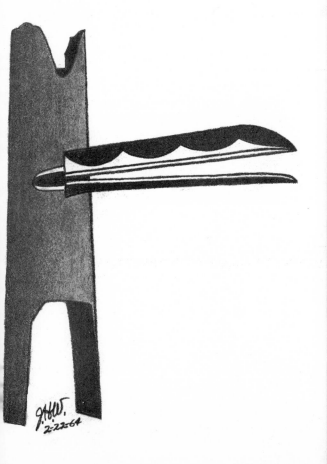

The Bella Coola and Tlingit generally cut the entire end of the log away for the entry; their poles were rarely over thirty feet high. The Kwakiutl, Nootka, and Coast Salish carved very few portal poles.

Occasionally a potlatch was given to celebrate the raising of one of these poles. In such an event, the guests were those who had assisted in building the house; the potlatch gifts they received were supplementary to the payment already made for their building services. The poles thus honored were also considered memorial in nature and were usually very tall.

The house-front pole was customarily surmounted by a crest. In the case of the Tlingit, the wife's family crest publicly proclaimed the dominant clan ruling the house. Always mounted against the house front, these hollowed semicircular logs did little to strengthen the house. In some instances valuables were concealed behind the carved surface. The taller the portal pole, the more powerful the owner.

Welcome figures were popular among the Nootka, moderately popular among the Kwakiutl but were raised only occasionally by the Coast Salish and seldom, if ever, by the more northern tribes. These figures were usually made by the assistants to the master carver. Rarely were they painted, and they seldom carried crests or other totem symbols. Installed at the edge of streams or salt water, they functioned as a sign of the waterfront sovereignty of the chief whose house property always included the beach.

At times of ceremony, the welcome figures marked the beach for the canoes of invited guests. To deface or steal one constituted an

As distinguished guests beached their canoes in anticipation of the impending potlatch in Nootka and Kwakiutl lands, they were greeted by realistic statues. Usually these welcome figures were of human form, often resembling the host. Rarely were such figures much more than life size, and those of this matched Nootka pair—about twelve feet tall —are the largest on the records of the British Columbia Government. The chief who had these figures carved must have given a bang-up potlatch of equally generous proportions, and he left no doubt in his guests' minds as to who owned the waterfront. These now stand near the Provincial Parliament buildings in Victoria's Thunderbird Park.

Looking something like cigar-store Indians, these are actually well but gaudily preserved welcome figures carved by a Quinault-Coast Salish carver. According to a former Quilliute Reservation resident, a subchief and his wife are represented. Note the tattooing on the faces of both figures and the chief's headdress, which is a representation of the aboriginal woven cedar-bark ceremonial regalia.

insult requiring a face-saving gesture, very likely armed attack on the offender. They were often placed in pairs, indicating that the shoreline between the two poles was personal as opposed to common clan property.

Mortuary poles were the rarest of all. Only the Haida used them to any great extent because of the cost in blankets and other goods. These were usually tall poles with cross boards. Very few remain and they are scattered widely. The clan crest invariably topped such poles. On the horizontal boards, covering the remains of a high-ranking chief, was his principal totem crest. The only example in the West is a reproduction in Thunderbird Park.

A few in unrestorable condition are still in isolated and overgrown ghost villages in Haida land. They were erected at special potlatches some time after funeral rites and usually stood some distance from the house in company with conventional memorial poles. Those of the southern Tlingit and coastal Tsimsyans were of inferior quality compared with those of the Haida.

Mortuary poles were a Haida specialty, but only a few are extant. This particular mortuary pole, which now stands in Victoria, British Columbia, is generally considered the finest of the few in existence. It is a precise duplicate of the rotted original that stood in the abandoned village of Tanu until 1911 when it was removed for copying. Eagle (clan crest) was perched above the horizontal front boards that once enclosed the remains of the chief in whose memory this pole was raised at a special potlatch. On the boards is an unusual rendition of Mountain Hawk, the chief's principal totem and a subcrest of Eagle clan. Below the boards is Raven (with broken beak); it is followed by a man's head wearing a three-section tall hat (skeels), meaning this chief had given three potlatches. Beaver (at bottom) has a small log clutched in his forepaws, and his usual crosshatched scaly tail and protruding incisor teeth.

In addition to these six widespread types of totem poles, special poles for special situations were sometimes raised. The Haida and Tlingit were the principal users of these strange and often ominous poles. Murder, adultery, kidnaping, robbery, unpaid obligations, and even counterfeiting of valuable "coppers" were but a few of the offenses prompting affluent chiefs

GRAVE TOTEMS KAKE

Because the Kake tribe of the Tlingit, though numbering only about 230 people in 1890, had a well-earned reputation for extracting double from those who had wronged them, the tallest pole (second from right) was erected as a grim warning—it was a "murder" pole! White man at the top was a constant reminder to Raven clansmen that one of their brothers had been killed, that his body rested uneasily beneath this pole. He could be avenged only with the lifeblood of two white men as several of his tribal brothers had been in recent years. Beneath White Man (a Russian) is his Kake victim, followed by Raven (the clan crest) as the avenging agent; the bottom figure, Halibut, represents the doomed murderer. The shorter totem next to the Russian Orthodox cross (some Kakes had converted) depicts a similar earlier murder. The two-symbol totem at the right shows a Raven crest variant (at the top) and Bear. (Winter & Pond)

to sound the summons for the services of a master carver to facilitate revenge.

This form of native justice, by means of visual advertising for all tribesmen and visitors to see, was almost always effective.

Several feuds, and even war, often resulted from the use of and desire for certain crests, with the Tlingit and northern or Kaigani-Haida sometimes making war on neighbors in order to capture crests and other symbols with particular appeal.

There were recognized types of poles for every purpose, and *they were all totem poles*, a point of controversy among ethnologists and anthropologists for decades. All types—even the ridicule and shame poles (and the murder pole)—fit the requirements: totem symbols and inherited or acquired crests graced all of these monuments to a race of wood artisans we are the poorer for not having recognized early enough to secure the preservation of more examples of their craft.

Chief Shaiks was the most influential Tlingit nobleman at the turn of the century. On Shaiks' Island, near Wrangell, Alaska, is a replica of a tribal dancing and feast house surrounded by restored poles. The most unusual of them is also the smallest and most easily overlooked—the T-shaped ridicule or shame pole (see below, far right, and drawing at left). Here's what happened! Three women of the neighboring Kiksadi tribe cohabited with three of Chief Shaiks' slaves. Finally tiring of housing and feeding the women, Shaiks demanded payment of the Kiksadi, whose chief refused responsibility. He said that he had disowned the women because they had brought shame to his tribe. In retaliation Chief Shaiks ordered three great frogs to be carved and mounted to ridicule the Kiksadi chief, whose personal totem was Frog. Three frogs for three no-good women! (Alaska Travel Division)

8

Making a Totem Pole

The social system of the Indians of the Northwest Coast was complicated and in many ways appears to have placed undue stress upon rank, whether earned or hereditary, and status within family, clan, and tribe. We moderns are inclined to accuse them of unwarranted ostentation, forgetting that upholding the class distinctions did require time, effort, and ingenuity. The otherwise simple life in an area of bountiful natural resources where securing the basic physical needs was a comparatively easy task would have left these Indians, in the aboriginal state, with time on their hands. Consequently, it was this inner compulsion to make one's mark that was responsible for the development of the plastic arts to a higher degree than was achieved anywhere else on the continent north of the Rio Grande.

An honest appraisal of their cultural developments shows that they were neither more immodest nor status prone than we are today. As tribes these Indians were all creative, and as individuals, they were never satisfied to duplicate exactly a neighbor's admired item. Every design or artifact showed some distinctive feature or improvement over a similar piece that had inspired the new work. If they had made automobiles, no two would have been alike in all details.

The possession of one's own totem pole, therefore, was a lifelong ambition, since the totem pole was the ultimate in status symbols. Being of a practical people, however, an owner raised his pole only after his family was securely housed and well fed. This equivalent of the Cadillac did not stand in front of a dwelling shabby by their standards, but graced the finest gabled house the owner could afford to construct with the primitive means available. So one had to have the ability to obtain worldly goods of trading or selling value and an already established reputation before one dared consider the ownership of a pole which was as much proof of status and wealth as it was a means of displaying family or tribal crests and picturing events of historical importance in one's lineage.

Thrift, then, was a virtue up to the point where wealth began to be obvious. Once such affluence was established, the Indian assumed a carefree attitude toward his capital goods, but, at the same time, determined to own a totem pole as indisputable evidence of his rising importance. Once he owned a totem pole—and the bigger, the better—his reputation and influence increased and power gravitated to him, regardless of his previous rank. The totem pole marked the man and, just as today, such possessions shed favorable rays on the nearest relatives who sometimes sought, undeservedly or not, to avail themselves of the influence and turn it to their own selfish advantage.

Generally speaking, the ownership of a large totem pole—the heraldic or memorial pole especially, often erected in honor of the present chief's predecessor—was reserved to chiefs of extended families and those of higher rank in the clan or tribe. After taking inventory of his accumulated possessions and their buying power, the chief looked about for a skilled and reputable carver. When the selected carver arrived, the chief and his advisers interviewed him to determine whether his spiritual experience and knowledge were equal to the exalted task. If he passed this test, the chief became his patron, and it was the wealth and power of these patrons that was largely responsible for the flourishing of the art that distinguished the maritime natives of the Northwest Coast.

If, on the other hand, the carver could not assure the chief as to his skill and knowledge, he was dismissed and another was summoned. Once a carver had satisfied the chief concerning his style and credentials, he was then often instructed by a shaman or one of the elders in the chief's household as to the detailed lineage and crests of the owner of the totem pole to be erected.

The duties and services of the chief's shaman and other advisers sometimes brought them sufficient wealth to enable them to acquire eventually totem poles of their own.

Carvers, too, often became as wealthy and as famous as many chiefs. Having completed an assignment, they were unrestricted in their movements and often journeyed to faraway places. Haida carvers who lived on the southern extremity of the Queen Charlotte Islands were retained by chiefs as far north as Prince of Wales Island, and Tsimsyan carvers living upriver on the Skeena and the Nass visited coastal tribes on lucrative assignments lasting months or a year or more. (As recently as 1912, carver Willie Clallam of Port Angeles, Washington, was called to Vancouver Island to carve a memorial pole for a Songhees Salish. This pole with its authentic, subdued colors now stands preserved in Thunderbird Park in Victoria, British Columbia.) Consequently, there is a marked similarity in style throughout the area although the tendency among the Tlingit, Haida, and Tsimsyan developed rapidly toward realism while that of the southern Kwakiutl, Bella Coola, Nootka, and Coast Salish tended to the grotesque. While these far-journeying woodcarvers spread the totem styles of one nation to another, they were invariably required to conform to the traditional styles of the customer's clan or tribe. A good carver, when finished with the pole, was paid the equivalent of up to seven hundred dollars or more.

Trained from youth by an uncle, or an unrelated carver of repute, a talented novice was steeped in the traditions of his clan and tribe. He had to learn all the spirit and medicine songs and dances and he was, therefore, at least theoretically, a devout person by the time he launched upon his own carving career. The apprentice carver in his youth had ceremonially cleansed himself and he had been properly initiated into most of the inner secrets of his family, clan, and tribal councils. Not only was a carver deeply spiritual in the usual sense, but he was—or was supposed to be—personally the protégé of one or more guardian spirits. In other words, no man could

Even during this century, carvers have been summoned from one tribal area to another. This Songhees-Salish memorial or heraldic pole was carved by Willie Clallam, a Port Angeles, Washington, Indian, for a fellow American Indian living near Victoria, British Columbia. The figures (from top down) are: Raven, Bear, Killer Whale, Man (possibly the owner) holding Lightning Snake mask, and Wolf.

hope to become a respected carver without deep spiritual insight. Such necessary attributes elevated him in the social structure from the start of his career. Skill with the tools of his trade was important, but his duties were of such proud and serious nature that his fame, after only a few successful carvings, spread far and wide. The wealthier the one seeking a carver, therefore, the finer the carver seeking the job and the higher his price. To be turned down for a position, which often took weeks and even months to negotiate, was a disgrace that could not be lived down quickly. Some great memorial poles are known to have taken a year and more to carve.

The fee was set when the customer and the carver came to complete agreement on other details, including a deadline for the completion of the task. In many respects the totem-pole carvers were the original free lancers on this continent, and meetings of carver and customer were somewhat analogous to modern conferences between an author and a publisher. Or we might say that the carver was in a position similar to that of a contractor bidding for a job to add another room to an owner's house. At any rate, the carver-customer relationship was an example of aboriginal private enterprise.

The owner of the pole-to-be, after the bargaining period (during which the customer was expected to provide for the daily wants of the carver), busied himself with the many political considerations attendant upon the important occasion. The shaman, on the other hand, devoted his energies to the spiritual aspects of the festivities that always accompanied the erection of a new pole.

The carver's first task was to select a suitable cedar tree as near as possible to the chosen site. If a tree could be found close to water, the task of moving it near the erection site was simplified: the tree, once felled, was stripped of its branches, split with the aid of stone or antler wedges, hollowed if large, floated to the village, and then dragged by manpower to a place convenient for the carving. On land heavy logs were moved about with the help of small rolling logs.

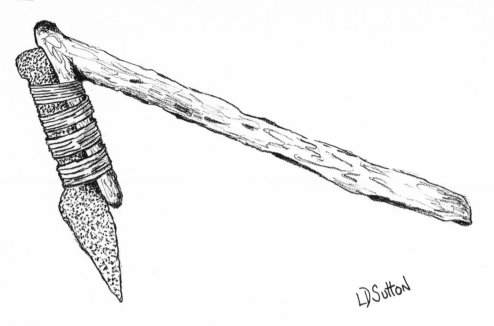

LDSutton

Stone adz with crabapple or other hardwood handle.

A Haida carver always used "medicine" in selecting a suitable tree. With his hands "doctored with medicine" and with a small piece of the heart of a yew tree in his mouth, he expected to be able to select a sound cedar. When his choice was made, he confirmed his judgment by cutting to the tree's heart.

The tools employed, before the arrival of the white man, were crude knives and adzes fashioned of stone or bone, and in the Far North of crude hammered copper. Fire was used by some carvers to facilitate hollowing a log. Before any carving was begun, the bark was stripped from the log and stored away to be used on house roofs or by the women of the owner's household in making ropes and mats, articles of clothing, and even blankets.

The heavy details of the faces, bodies, and limbs of the animal-like symbols were carved boldly. The minor details, such as the mouths and eyes, were achieved more painstakingly with short, brisk strokes of the cutting tool. Chisels of stone and bone were used with mallet-like hammers made of crab-apple wood boiled to make it harder. One indication of a

pole's authentic native origin is the appearance of infinite small concave surface cuts made by the adz. Of course this cannot be a general rule because some modern carvers, who usually possess only a smattering of the ancient lore, have managed to duplicate the small surface cuts. The hatchetlike adz in all sizes, either with a pointed blade or a nearly straight cutting edge, was used with great skill as were primitive gouges and scrapers. Some early carvers on the Northwest Coast used the rough skin of sharks as a primitive but effective substitute for sandpaper which was, of course, unknown to them. With the arrival of the early white traders, iron and steel tools were obtained in exchange for beaver, marten, and sea-otter pelts. The adz, now steel, is still the most efficient cutting tool.

Because the specific design of many of the crests and other symbols were the private property of the owner of the pole being carved, secrecy was usually provided by screening the pole from public view during carving. In Haida land, the chief's confidants inspected each symbol as it was being carved

One of the very few moderns to have successfully mastered the ancient totem-carving art is Mark Westby, a non-Indian, of Seattle. While in La Push, Washington, Westby lived so closely with the Quilliutes that they shared their ancient lore with him. He is shown here beside the cottage in which he lived while he studied with the Quilliutes. The miniature totem pole is one of Westby's own making—a Wolf clan pole. Note the adz marks. The mask, however, is an original (not a copy) ceremonial dance mask.

on the pole; the carving had to conform precisely to clan traditions and customs. Some carvers made patterns of animal skins before doing any actual carving on the hollowed half-log, the walls of which were about five to ten inches thick.

Among the Tsimsyan and Tlingit tribes, a "committee" of elders was in charge of the carver. These elders from the maternal, or "opposite," clan of the chief, were fed and housed during the entire time of carving, after which they were liberally remunerated. Similar protocol prevailed among the nations farther south. A shaman was often included in the overseeing group and incantations and much "medicine" were employed.

Probably the most highly trained and paid of all carvers were those of the Kitka'ata and Wudstae Tsimsyan, who fell into two distinct classes: the *gitsontk* ("people who are secluded") and the ordinary carvers, who, though efficient, were not of superior skill. The Tsimsyan *gitsontk*, who were often retained for important carving tasks by distant tribes, did their work in complete secrecy and carved only the symbols of guardian spirits (*narhnorh* in Tsimsyan). Trained from childhood in this most honored of all carving duties, the *gitsontk* could demand the death penalty as punishment for anyone who intruded or spied upon them at work. By the same means the *gitsontk* were disposed of for making the slightest error.

Aside from their totem-pole carvings, these spirit carvers of the Northern Tsimsyan contrived some wondrous inventions, which they were required to operate during public ceremonies or in warfare. Sometimes disaster was the result. One such display is described by Marius Barbeau in a bulletin of the National Museum of Canada published some years ago. Barbeau relates how a Wudstae *gitsontk* who lived near the frontier of the Kwakiutl nation invented a large whalelike affair. Made of wood, and being hollow, this "whale" is said in ancient stories to have been able to swim and dive and spout water. Inside the whale's body was a compartment large enough to accom-

modate several warriors. Now Killer Whale was considered an evil spirit by all of the Northwest Indians. Whale and his cousin, Blackfish, had great power and were feared because they often overturned the dugouts of fishing parties. The *gitsontk* reasoned that his wonderful creation, because it looked exactly like a whale, could have a decisive effect in the event of battle near a waterside enemy village. Used with proper strategy, it could, he believed, cause great consternation among unsuspecting foes.

Because the contraption performed well on its first public showing and because his tribesmen were impressed by its possibilities, the *gitsontk* decided to try it out under combat conditions. He would simulate a night attack—a sort of aboriginal drill for a proposed amphibious operation at a later date against the Kwakiutl. With an enthusiastic crowd watching from the shore, the *gitsontk* and his invisible crew approached. In the light of the flickering fires, the watchers were suddenly dismayed to see the primitive control mechanism, which operated the whale's tail, go haywire. The whale floundered and the *gitsontk*, thoroughly disgraced and knowing well that his fate would be summary execution, immediately took a purposeful leap into the inky water and drowned. The crew in the whale's belly was not seen again either; the mechanical whale probably filled quickly with water and the hapless assistants shared the fate of the *gitsontk*.

Many carvers, including the highly skilled *gitsontk*, were often honored by being admitted to the sacred circle of advisers to chiefs who were themselves of sufficiently high rank to be admitted to the secret tribal councils. Such fortunate carvers sometimes accompanied their chiefs on distant journeys; occasionally they were sent as couriers on secret missions of state. Thus their position in the caste-ridden culture was often immediately below that of the chief and shaman in that order—a great honor, indeed, for a sculptor.

To return to the actual carving of the totem pole, the Indians had difficult problems in ad-

The carving of ceremonial masks was the talented artist's means of attracting attention. An aspirant to a career as a totem-pole carver sometimes spent his spare time in such small tasks. The surface of this ceremonial mask depicting Bear appears to have been smoothed, possibly with sharkskin, and the teeth are real. (Courtesy Lowie Museum of Anthropology, University of California, Berkeley)

dition to those of working with primitive tools. They lacked pigments as we moderns know them, and they lacked preservatives, but they had been favored by Providence with one of the most durable of all woods, and one of the easiest to carve. Stripped of its bark, the bare, smooth surface of a tall red cedar was also a fine basic color for the background. When weathered, the red cedar assumes an attractive silvery shade. However, this tree does not grow to outsize heights much farther north than Latitude 57 degrees. Therefore, the Far Northern totem-pole carvers, if a tall pole was required, had to secure long logs from tribes farther south. In such an event, a considerable crew with a large dugout had to venture south and tow the log through the often treacherous waters of the coastal areas now a part of British Columbia and Southeastern Alaska. Because of the difficulties this entailed, cottonwood was sometimes used for the tallest poles in the north country, despite its being harder to carve, not as durable, and thus a rather poor substitute.

The old poles, and the authentically preserved ones which have been restored as nearly as possible or practicable to their original condition, were *not* painted in the garish and blatant glossy colors so frequently employed today to attract unsuspecting tourists. Charcoal, manganese, or graphite mixed with fish or animal oils, or ground dry and fine with salmon eggs well chewed to liquid consistency, produced either black or various shades of gray. Solid browns, reds, or whites were obtained by mixing ochers of those colors. Reds from pinks to dark hues were made by mixing various berries or animal blood with oils. A fungus growth common to the northern hemlock, when decayed, gave a bright yellow, and the southern Tlingit also made yellow by mixing *sekhone* moss with various oils. Light brown was obtained by mixing bear dung with chewed cedar bark and oils. For green, the Indians turned to the copper-bearing rocks. These were vigorously scraped, the greenish flakes powdered and mixed with animal fats and oils to make a fine green. Blue was difficult, but purple was rather easily obtained from dark berries that grew profusely in the entire Pacific Northwest region, which was dotted with rain forests.

A carver usually did his own painting, although he sometimes had an assistant, in which case the apprentice occupied himself in obtaining the materials, mixing them in stone dishes, and applying the colors. He also made the brushes or daubs from strands of fine cedar bark or of animal fur.

While the carver was busy with his artistic endeavors, another talented person, the songwriter, was equally engaged in producing the entertainment and ceremonials for the great event, the potlatch. He, too, had been retained by the pole's owner and his selection was as exacting as the carver's had been. He was invariably a kinsman or a member of the chief's clan or tribe. As soon as he and the chief had agreed on the price he was to obtain for his work, he began gathering singers and warriors and squaws with acting and dancing abilities. Deep in the forests the performers were trained and rehearsed for long hours over periods as long as several weeks or months. So great an event was the potlatch, that little room for mistakes was allowed either the songwriter or his performers. For a successful production, though, they could count on a generous payment. To produce a flop or embarrass the chief in the potlatch could easily bring about a songwriter's end.

The shaman, again acting on behalf of the chief, worked closely with the songwriter to insure strict adherence to the religious doctrines of the clan or tribe and to make certain that the songs—composed especially for the coming potlatch—correctly told the stories of the chief's family, their exploits and origins. To insult favored guardian spirits would be ill-advised and no means was spared to insure the blessings of the Supreme Being. Songwriters gained great prominence in the Northwestern societies and their services were widely sought. Unfortunately, the talents required for composing suitable anthems and songs to accompany the many spirit dances were more easily acquired than was carving ability. The supply thus more closely approximating the demand, songwriters were not generally as highly remunerated as were the carvers. Their responsibilities were, however, as great, and their punishment, if they failed, was severe. It was cause for banishment or reduction to slave status if the songwriter failed faithfully to tell of all the chief's accomplishments and to relate precisely the history of his family and clan. The greater the responsibility, the greater the punishment for unfaithful service.

While these two artists were thus busied with sculpturing and theatrical productions—and the latter invariably took on grandiose proportions—the women of the chief's household, assisted by the slaves if he owned any, were preparing to feed the hordes of invited relatives and guests from far and near due to arrive just a day or two after the agreed deadline for the completion of the totem pole and songs. The more important the guest, the greater the numbers of slaves and relatives in his retinue. The womenfolk, therefore, had to prepare large quantities of smoked salmon, venison, caribou (in the case of the northernmost tribes), bear meat, berries, tasty roots, cakes made of dried wild fruit, and the like. Especially popular was "squaw candy," braided strips of smoked salmon. It can still be obtained in the Far North and the author attests to its succulence. The amounts of food and drink, including the zesty and alcoholic *soop-a-lallie*, made of a brew of mixed soapberries and eulachon oil with fresh water, was staggering. Equally staggering, on many occasions, was the feasting at the potlatch.

Whether or not the totem pole was ready as the time for the influx of guests approached determined the happiness or ill-fortune of the carver; similarly that of the songwriter. The host, too, faced ruin and loss of face if the timing was not perfect. Organization counted!

9

The Great Potlatch

The Indians of the Northwest Coast never suffered regionwide war with the whites as did their brothers of the continental expanse to the southeast. Easily applied to them, too, however, was the brutal philosophy of General Philip Sheridan's cynical observation of 1869— "The only good Indians I ever saw were dead"—and with similarly tragic results. By discouraging and sometimes forcibly suppressing the practice of the Indians' greatest institution, the whites finally destroyed the natives' *esprit de corps*.

Discrediting the potlatch as an institution was a monumental infringement of their social and cultural rights and an outstanding example of failure to understand them. This viewpoint will be clarified as we examine the multifaceted and interrelated aspects of this colorful event, one of the last of which was held in Wrangell in 1940—a rather anemic affair with little of the ancient flavor.

The word potlatch is a corruption of the Nootka *patshatl*, which went, via the Chinook jargon, into general West Coast usage. In the process the true meaning of this word has become grossly confused. Correctly interpreted, *patshatl* means "a gift" or "a gift giving" in essence, but the event was much more in actual aboriginal intent and practice.

The idea persists, even among well-educated people, that the traditional potlatch of the Pacific Northwest Indians was nothing more than an ostentatious display of wealth and a wasteful giveaway of valuables followed by an orgy of licentiousness and consumption of enormous quantities of alcohol. Ostentatious they were, and often boisterous—but so is the Mardi Gras in our allegedly enlightened civilization. In contrast, the potlatch had depth of purpose.

The potlatch of the old days was primarily a time for pridefully recounting one's heritage,

Charlie Tagcock, a professional carver and one of the few remaining, carved this totem pole for Wrangell businessmen, which, in 1940, was erected on the main street. Everyone was invited to a fair attempt at an old-time potlatch, but modern surroundings spoiled the effect. A towering, sixty-five feet tall, the pole records (from top down) the tale of Raven bringing light into the world, a traditional Tlingit Grampus (Killer Whale) story, and the saga of the Cannibal Giant Goo-teekhl. The small face on Goo-teekhl (see bottom of pole) is Mosquito. (Pacific Northern Airlines)

for celebrating clan or tribal independence, of confirmation, introduction, of commencement upon new responsibilities, recognition, and memorial day rolled into one great and glorious experience to be remembered for a lifetime.

The traditional gift giving was important, but it was incidental to the primary objectives and was, in fact, payment for various services rendered the host. The entire protocol was quite like that observed today in official government circles and in upper-crust social events.

If the organizational skill of the host, his councilors and kinsmen, and the efficiency of the womenfolk and servants of his clan or group was up to par, all was in readiness for the arrival of the guests on the appointed day. In Nootka, Kwakiutl, and the fringe of Coast Salish country, welcome figures marked the host's beach. Farther north the host chiefs usually met their highest-ranking guests personally or stationed subordinates at the water's edge as official greeters. In the latter case, the chief, in regal splendor, frequently occupied the grade, beside his principal house post immediately in front of the painted screen which secluded his personal apartment.

The canoes bearing guests sometimes rendezvoused offshore displaying their individual house and clan crests. Landing was in order of rank, the occupants of each vessel stepping ashore with dignity and strict regard for personal position. In ancient times slaves of the host were occasionally clubbed to death and their bodies used as rollers to facilitate beaching a particularly powerful chief's canoe. This demonstrated the wealth of the host chief; he had resources to spare.

Even the size of the arriving canoes was significant: the larger the canoe, the greater the chief and the more people in his retinue. The more spacious the vessel, the greater too was its gift-carrying capacity. Each occupant's traveling kit included eating implements—bowls, grease box, ladles and spoons, baskets, cooking utensils (the journey was often long)—and personal adornments. In the old days slaves paddled the canoes, toted luggage,

and performed menial chores. Late arrivals were infrequent because tardiness resulted in loss of face for the guest and was an insult to the host and his entire lineage. Everyone, host and guest alike, was supposed to be on his best behavior.

The weary guests, often a hundred miles or more from their own villages, were officially presented to their host. The initial amenities over, the guests were directed to the feasting area, in which cooking boxes bubbled and game boiled or roasted in the open. Bowls were filled with delicacies, eulachon oil was poured into each guest's box, and the baskets carried by children were loaded with berry cakes. Spirits were raised and appetites sharpened by the zippy and frothy *soop-a-lallie* and, depending upon the program, the remainder of the first day was devoted to renewing old friendships and meeting new friends, recounting ancient tales, enjoying games of chance, watching dramatic performances, and—naturally—more feasting. For the host to serve insufficient or bad food or for a guest to indicate displeasure at the food served, and the entertainment provided, was considered sufficiently insulting to merit retaliation—a raid by a war party perhaps, or worse yet, being stricken from the guest list for the next potlatch.

All needs of the guests, often a hundred or more, were provided by the host with the exception of sleeping blankets and personal items. The chief's house was large and easily accommodated guests of high rank. Less important people slept outside in the shelter of the walls or in a temporary lean-to of cedar bark and branches. Careened canoes provided additional shelter from the elements.

The merriment generally lasted several days. Around blazing fires, made more spectacular with dousings of oil, the guests vied with one another far into the night, telling stories of adventures and of thrilling encounters with supernatural beings. Visiting chiefs would enviously conjecture as to the possible size and grandeur of the pole that was to be raised.

Meanwhile the symbol of the festive gather-

These three typical Northwest Coast Indian baskets come from the Olympic Peninsula, where they were woven, circa 1907, by a member of one of the Coast Salish tribes—possibly the Quinault. Tightly woven of spruce roots, the one on the left is watertight. The center basket is a typical container for uncooked foods. On the right is a native adaptation using salt-grass over white man's wire, but the weaving technique is authentic. These baskets are the property of the author's mother.

ing—the recently completed totem pole—remained in guarded seclusion. For a guest to view it before the appointed time was unthinkable. But that time was known only to the host chief and his councilors.

After the passing of an interval well calculated to arouse the curiosity of the guests to high pitch, the chief or his "speaker" would make a formal announcement.

The time for the raising of the new totem pole was at hand!

Immediately the guests were seated—in order of rank—they struck up a rhythmic haw-haw-haw-haw interspersed with ho-ho-ho to the accompaniment of drums and rattles.

Presently, amid increased fanfare, the pole-raising crew (escorted by the councilors responsible for the carver's work) appeared carrying or dragging the carved log with the figures facing the sky. Exceptionally long and heavy poles were maneuvered into place by using smaller logs as rollers. (A few chiefs in ancient times are said to have tossed a slave or two—thoroughly clubbed—into the post hole as proof of affluence but *not* as a human sacrifice as many early Europeans erroneously believed.) When the base of the pole was positioned in the prepared trench and hole, the chanting reached its peak.

Stout ropes of woven cedar bark or strips of animal hide were attached to the pole and flung over a leverage log. The crew stood by

Tlingit Indians sit according to rank in a modernized version of a traditional house. Note the contrast between the new (microphone for a public address system) and the old, typified by ancient-style rattles, robes with suspect semi-totem symbols, a typical feathered headdress, and what may be a shaman's mask (see man in center). (Alaska Travel Division)

while the free end of the rope was grasped by guests in a gesture combining friendship with recognition of the exalted position of the host. At a prearranged signal—given by the host or one appointed to act in his behalf—all hands strained to raise the great monument to the vertical while the spectators shouted acclamation and trained singers added their voices to the general din.

The pole trench was filled in immediately and the earth firmly stomped, usually by the dancers who had anxiously awaited the signal for their appearance. In some tribes, slaves provided the muscle. Then the ropes, which had detracted from the grace of the pole, were cut away and the new possession stood in all its glory. Expressions of acclamation were heard and ranking guests often arose in admiration.

Amid the happy tumult an occasional disparaging grunt or insulting remark was overheard. Such effrontery could mean only that the perpetrator was contemptuous of the new pole—inferior to his own perhaps—and consequently deemed the host of questionable influence and power. Kinsmen of the host would note such insults: they would be rectified later by "ordeals" or war unless restitution was rendered promptly. Frequently tallies were made of approval and dissent.

Once the pole was in place, the chief, or his speaker, stepped forward. The smart rapping of the "talking stick" or "speaker's staff" brought silence, for this was the moment of supreme importance. Raising the pole had been exciting, but now all present would hear and witness the several reasons for the great potlatch.

The orator of the moment, the chief or his speaker, stood erect in full regalia with the ceremonial braided cedar bark and eagle-down headdress. As this was the high point of the formal ceremony, the speech would elaborately describe each crest and figure on the new pole.

Let us imagine ourselves as honored guests

"In the old days" the Indians raised their totem poles with a remarkable knowledge of leverage and tackle. The method was almost identical to that used by the Maoris of New Zealand.

Chilkat-Tlingit young people show great interest in preserving the traditions of their ancestors. A handsome people, these ceremonial dancers are wearing authentic Chilkat robes (not blankets), totem-decorated dance leggings, and masks portraying supernatural beings such as Hawk, Squid, Eagle Mother, and Wolf. (Alaska Travel Division)

at a potlatch long ago—before the Europeans came. . . .

Comfortably seated on woven cedar-bark mats spread on the grassy slope in front of the great house of the Clan of the Wolves in Kitwancool, we chiefs—and I am the least—are honored guests. This is the land of the ancient and autonomous Gitksan tribe and we are in Tsimsyan land. We are about one hundred miles up the Skeena River on the tributary Ks-

gin-daa-hin, a creek through which flows the pure, sweet waters of the lake bearing the name of our host's tribe. The tangy mountain air is good in our lungs and adds zest to the pungent soapberry brew in our wooden totem cups. We are free men, rich with nature's endowments. Our women's shoulders, are covered with warm Chilkat capes which we received in trade from a Kaigani-Haida carver last year near the Skeena's mouth after a Gitrhahla potlatch.

One of the few authentic "talking sticks" or "speakers' staffs" existing is this superb and valuable example. Of Kaigani-Haida origin, this staff (only the upper quarter of the five-foot staff is shown) is believed to be well over one hundred years old. The figures (from top down) are Eagle, Grampus (Killer Whale), and Wolf. (Courtesy Phoebe Hearst Collection, Lowie Museum of Anthropology, University of California, Berkeley)

"Hark, my husband," comes the whispered warning from my wife. "Wolf Chief Gam-gak-men-muk, our host, will have us witness what Speaker says."

We are quiet, for we are about to repay our host for the fine feasting, entertainment, and lodgings we have enjoyed these past few days. In return for our witness, there also will be gifts before Sun reaches the edge of the world where West Wind dwells.

"Look upon my chief's new pole," Speaker begins. "Is it not marvelous? Carver has indeed done a great work and he has received many skins of the land otter and a canoe box of goat-hair blankets trimmed with marten skins of a number equal to a moon. Carver is well paid for his fine work.

"My host's high rank is evident for, as head chief of his clan he sits here in the middle with the second Wolf chief at his right hand, the third chief at his left, the fourth chief at his right, and the young fifth chief at his left. Wolf Chief wears his crest in front; it is trimmed with ermine skins and his hat is filled with the down of Eagle. Later the down will shower on you in friendship.

"I, We-dak-hai-yatzqu (big copper), Head Chief of Frog Clan of the Kitwancool, am honored to be Speaker. I know this story is true: it confirms Wolf Chief's heritage and his right to the ownership and power of the crests and to the lands of his people."

The speaker, a great chief of rank and privileges equal to our host (or he would not be Speaker), pauses. As a young subchief who only two years ago inherited my uncle's authority and position, this is only my second experience as an honored potlatch guest. I have ushered at my uncle's three potlatches, confirmed by the three-section *ksahlanemrait* on one of his poles. I must listen intently so that when I give my first potlatch at Neeslaranows, I will know the lineage of my host—who will be my guest—and treat him with the respect he deserves, for his clan and tribe have never been conquered and, they say, they never will be.[1] I am especially honored, for not always does a Gitksan chief invite other Wolves—even of another Tsimsyan tribe—to his great potlatch.

These thoughts race through my mind as I gaze upon the splendor of the spectacle before me. But hark!

"Hear me, honored guests," Speaker shouts, raising his totem staff high. "This pole's name is Skim-sim and Will-a-daugh, after the large bird beneath the house carvings [miniatures] near the top of the pole and the mother and child near the base. On top of the pole is Wee-get-weltku [Giant Woodpecker], a powerful spirit, for he watches over the forest and plumbs the depths of the red cedar to make certain the heartwood is sound. The small people of Gilt-winth [the Wolf clan] are above Will-a-daugh and her child."

It occurs to me that this is a most curious order, for the most important crest is usually at the top, yet Will-a-daugh and her child are at the bottom. But I remind myself that the customs of the Kitwancool are as admirable as their tenacity and independence, and they have a right to them, for this is their historic land.

"Six hundred years ago the Clan of the Wolves had their village at Ke-an [present day Prince Rupert, B.C.].[2] One day, while

[1] As of this writing the sturdy Kitwancool have not treated with the Canadian Government or bargained away their ancient lands. They live at peace, however, and their tribal autonomy is observed.

[2] The legends related in this imaginary Kitwancool potlatch some four hundred years ago are from material gratefully obtained from Dr. Wilson Duff, curator of the Provincial Museum at Victoria, B.C. The Kitwancool say the beginning of their historic migration was some "one thousand years ago."

This fine old Tlingit totem pole has been disfigured by conscienceless vandalism—an old painted tin can with seam showing at front has been fitted over the three-sectioned hat that means the clan elder (top figure) had given three potlatches. Below clan elder is Wolf as a clan crest and what appears to be Whale with a human visage. (Alaska Travel Division)

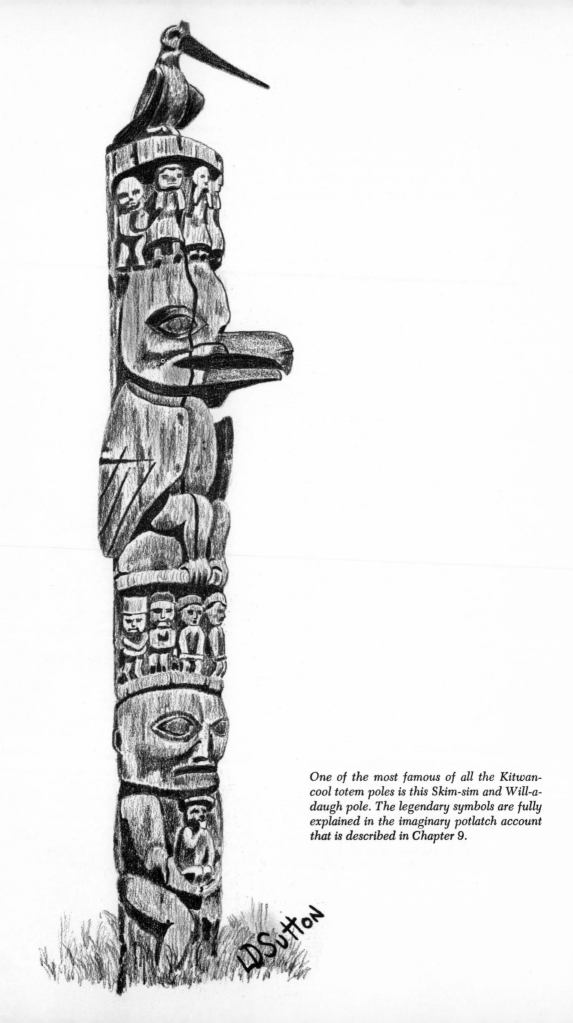

One of the most famous of all the Kitwan-cool totem poles is this Skim-sim and Will-a-daugh pole. The legendary symbols are fully explained in the imaginary potlatch account that is described in Chapter 9.

out gathering wood, the chief's beautiful niece met a supernatural wood grub, with whom she fell in love. In due time she bore a child and laid it in a cradle by the wall of the chief's great house. The princess sang many a *lim-ath-a-now* [lullaby]. One day the wood-grub child ate its way through the wall. Before its mother, the niece of the chief, was aware of what had happened, the child had burrowed through the ground to the next dwelling in which it ate everything made of wood. The child ate and burrowed through many houses and the people were alarmed.

"But because the wood-grub child was part spirit and part human, only one part of it was doing this. Finally the people in the last house heard a noise, and opening one of their boxes, they discovered a giant wood grub. Quickly they attacked it. Then they saw they were stabbing only *a part* of the grub and they followed its huge body. They had to dig a ditch and as they dug they kept stabbing and cutting at the wood grub with their weapons. Soon they had dug a trench right back to the cradle by the wall in the house of the chief.

"To this day this ditch can be seen in Ke-an by those who know this story and where to look. Of course the niece of the chief was heartbroken. She wished that the water would flood over the village to take revenge on the people who had destroyed her baby. The water did rise, but only the grieving mother, Will-a-daugh, was drowned.

"Now the people wanted to leave Ke-an, so the chief led the clan to the Nish-gah [Nass River], where they built houses and called their new village An-lath-gauth-u. This means 'able to see two directions.' One day the chief led a party of hunters into the mountains. Presently a *queak-u* [groundhog] said 'hea-uk' several times to a young hunter, which meant 'she is at it again.' The young hunter knew at this that his wife was not faithful. Quickly he ran to the village and to the outside wall of his apartment. Pulling the boards apart was easy, for they were fastened with roots in the ancient manner. The *queak-u* was right, for in his bed with his wife was a stranger.

"After the young man had killed his rival, he picked up the robe and saw that it was trimmed with marten and ermine skins. Obviously his wife's lover was the son of a powerful chief. Who could he have been?"

We shake our heads in wonder. This is truly an exciting history. But listen. . . .

"The dead man's robe was decorated, around the bottom, with the precious hoofs of unborn caribou. Even today a duplicate is a valuable ceremonial robe of the Clan of the Wolves.

"The chief arrived, picked up the robe, and then he heard a distant voice calling in anguish. It was Will-a-daugh, now a supernatural bird, who was mother of the dead man—the supernatural prince of the wolves; he had been only masquerading as a human. He owned two names, Ga-ba-gam-kwen and Gam-gak-men-muk. The first name meant the 'man who killed and ate ten deer at a time,' and the second name meant 'man who bit off the ears of the deer and ate them.' The second name is very valuable—worth hundreds of feasts—and is the hereditary name of the chief of the Gilt-winth, your host, who sits rightfully and proudly here at the center of his subchiefs."

We nod our heads in affirmation, for everyone knows that a name of supernatural origin is indeed of inestimable value. But who does the biggest bird figure on the great new pole represent?

"On the new pole," Speaker was saying as if in answer to the question on my lips, "is the symbol of the mother of the supernatural wolf prince. She is Will-a-daugh, the niece of the ancient chief in Ke-an, who drowned and became a supernatural bird when her wood-grub child was killed. From her the Wolf clan obtained its funeral song so long ago when, as the chief held the valuable robe of the dead wolf prince and looked up to the sky, the mother flying high over the village cried, of her new bereavement, 'Give me back my son, Lou-see-tee-au, Lou-see-tee-au, lqu-lquu.' This is the death song yet today of the head chief of the Wolf clan."

Now Speaker waved his staff high again.

"'If you do not give me back my son, something terrible will happen,' cried the supernatural Mountain Eagle, mother of the wolf prince. At this warning the chief told the young hunter to return her dead son's robe.

"When the great bird refused this offer, Gwass-lam, the chief, put the robe on the roof of his house. But this failed too and as the bird kept flying, she sang the death song and, presently, a terrible rainstorm came and almost washed away the whole village.

"Then the chief ordered his people to move farther up the river to a new place they called Zam-an-lu-tool, which means 'safe or protected river.' While the chief and his people explored this new place, they set up camp by a spring of pure water.

"One day something mysterious was seen in the water. The chief's nephews brought out a carved box. They did not know what it was.

"Then they heard a wailing voice warning them. As in their last village, it was the supernatural Skim-sim, the Mountain Eagle mother, Will-a-daugh, crying for her dead son. The voice threatened to make something awful happen again. Then Chief Gwass-lam decided the box looked like a house built over a pit in rock; each corner was carved with a figure of Bear. While the grieving mother kept crying threats, the chief held the box over the fire.

"At this gesture the crying ceased and the bird mother said that nothing would happen as she then had her child. The chief kept the box with its name dhak-gam-loab, and today it is a crest of the Clan of the Wolves."

My thoughts tell me this box contained the spirit of the dead prince of the wolves. It reminds me of Raven's "box holding light" at the beginning of the world. But . . .

"Chief Gwass-lam had his people move again; this time they traveled to Git-an-yow, right here in this place, and this name means 'big village.' Fifteen miles long the village was in those days. After many wars with the Tse-tsaut people, who are not Tsimsyan but came from the East, our people became few so they changed their name to 'Kitwancool' which means 'narrow valley.'

"In those long ago days, the houses were so huge that two smoke holes were needed to let the smoke out. The small figures beneath Giant Woodpecker were the house carvings. One house was named An-wi-sin-zock, which means 'large.' Strangers entering the door were zoak [embarrassed] because they had so far to walk to the back of the house.

"The crests used on this pole were brought from Ke-an six hundred years ago," said Speaker with a triumphant wave of his staff. "All present have already witnessed the custom of the Kitwancool which is to erect a new pole when the old one has decayed. It is always erected in the same place, and a great feast is held. This is such a feast so that all Wolves will know their lands, their hunting grounds, where to fish, and each generation will know what they own and the history and lineage of their clan."

All our heads nodded in agreement as Speaker told of the lands of the Wolf clan and explained the tribe's territories.

Then Chief Gam-gak-men-muk, hereditary owner of the ancient supernatural name, passed near us, and the eagle down fell among us in friendship and peace. Then while we feasted again, the servants of the chief gathered the gifts we would receive after we witnessed more important happenings.

And so progressed the multifaceted program on the last day of a potlatch typical of the old days. After another sumptuous feast, the guests reassembled. Children playing on the beach and among the long canoes were called to sit quietly and learn more. Some of the Wolf clan youngsters were scheduled to be presented during the next few hours.

Presently, with great shouts, singers reappeared along with leaping dancers. They would reenact the great events Speaker had explained before the sun stood high; there would be spirit songs and dances so the guests would understand all they had been told.

Finally the chief gave a signal. A nephew, recently having reached maturity, was brought forth, carrying two fine masks and miniatures of four valuable coppers. Being the

These Kitwancool totem poles, in Kispiox, British Columbia (eight miles north of Hazel-ton), are very possibly around one hundred years old. This ancient tribe claims their poles remain erect up to two hundred years. (British Columbia Government)

An authentic Chilkat-Tlingit spirit dancing group prepares to portray an ancient ritual on the grounds of a semiauthentic tribal community house. If the planks were mounted vertically, this house would look ancient indeed. The house-front painting portrays the ancient supernatural Raven, the spirit being who "brought light to the world in the beginning." (Alaska Travel Division)

oldest nephew, the young man was publicly invested with a heredity name and officially designated as successor to the present head chief. From this time forth the young heir would sit at council meetings and receive advanced instruction in all the clan and tribal history. On the death of his uncle, he would assume his title and robes, his crest and great coppers. Ultimately, after interment of the late chief, he would hold a memorial potlatch. The clan would start now to save a store of

goods with which to pay a carver for the future pole that would be raised to him.

The priests of the clan then appeared, and while the dancers and singers performed the spirit ceremonies, children approaching puberty were initiated into secret societies. Among the Haida, smaller children were led away to secluded places and tattooed, with clan elders, an important guest as witness, and shamans officiating. In many tribes the ears of small girls and boys were pierced for pendants, and lower lips or noses were pierced for valuable labrets.

Thus were the proud offspring of commoners and nobility alike formally introduced to potlatch guests who were witnesses to their "commencement" into increasing responsibilities.

Talents were recognized: an aspirant to a career as a totem carver would be accepted as an assistant by a master craftsman; a boy or girl who had experienced spirit power and perception was taken under the tutelage of a healer or a prominent shaman.

Sometimes coppers worth many thousands

These Haida masks were once used in the great winter dances. On the left mask the eye designs might indicate that it belonged to a man whose guardian spirit was Eagle. On the mask at the right the eyes are of Wolf; the faintly perceptible painted inverted feathers across the face almost certainly combine with the eyes to indicate the monster Sea Wolf Wasgo; a small Frog crest is on top of the head. The four miniature coppers were often used on ceremonial costumes and represented actual large coppers. (Courtesy Phoebe Hearst Collection, Lowie Museum of Anthropology, University of California, Berkeley)

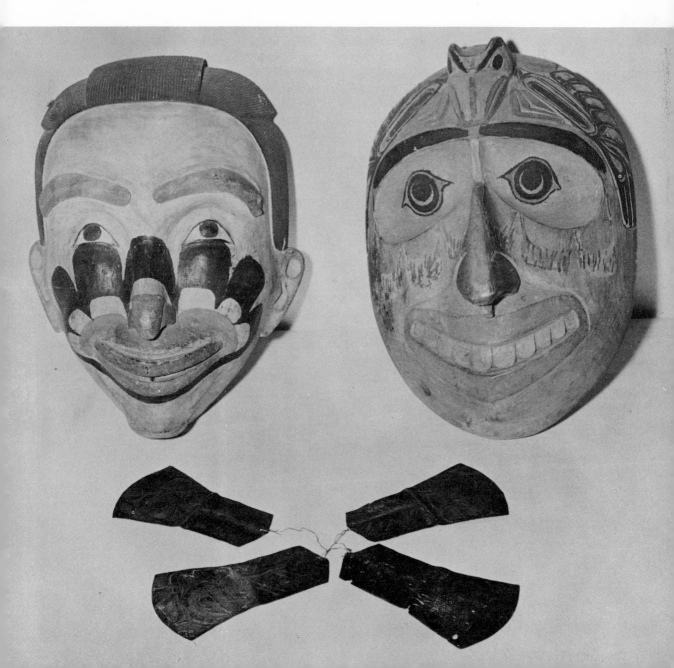

of dollars—in today's currency—were sold or dramatically exhibited. And throughout the gala day the singers and dancers, who had been drilled for months, displayed their combined abilities, and special performances showed the masks and treasured spirit devices of the host chief's house.

When the time for gifts arrived, the guests, in order of rank, received blankets, robes, capes, and sometimes weapons and tools.

After Hudson's Bay posts were established at Fort Rupert, Port Simpson, at Bella Coola, and on Vancouver Island, when the Russians and finally Americans first pioneered the Alaskan panhandle, guns and iron blades for the adz, as well as other tools, became valuable potlatch gifts.

There were highly specialized potlatches, too: an insult or an injustice was often rectified by the perpetrator's inviting guests to witness that the wronged person received the first and largest gift. Sometimes even this justifiable partiality caused hard feelings.

Funeral potlatches were not unlike a modern wake. There was mourning and skillful performances describing the adventurous life of the deceased chief. Among some tribes, this event combined the introduction of the successor to the mantle of the deceased's authority and the assumption of the prerogatives, crests, and privileges of his inherited rank. In such instances, the heir was the actual host.

The building of a new and larger house called for a special potlatch. Generally the "opposites"—the clansmen of the consort of the host chief—were retained to build the new dwelling. Of course, this required a new housefront pole and some new house posts, so again the best carver the chief could afford had been summoned.

Victory potlatches were held to celebrate a successful war against an enemy, and often, particularly in Haida country, a similar celebration was held after a triumphant trade voyage or slave raid down the coast to Chinook country or to northern California.

The remarkably powerful Haida and southern Tlingit chiefs frequently gave valuable slaves as gifts, while the Nootka—the masters of all in canoe design and building—found their great craft especially desirable gift items.

For a guest to sulk and drag a gift like blankets on the ground meant he was insulted: his host had embarrassed him by giving him a picayunish present. After all, he had taken much time for the journey to witness the proceedings at this potlatch. His presence was worth more than the rags tendered. He would raid his ungrateful host's village; maybe he would give a greater potlatch. In the latter event, his current host, despite his rank, would receive his gift last and, instead of otter skins or marten-trimmed blankets, he would receive only two or three mountain-goat skins, possibly no more than a woven cedar-bark cape or a pair of worn-out dance leggings. The offended one might even decide to erect a ridicule pole at a potlatch! He'd get even.

There were smaller special potlatches for marriages, for reaching puberty, and smaller ones still (but the biggest the host could afford) when a baby ate his first solid food—to celebrate obtaining spirit power—and for any other reason imaginable when the clan wealth permitted. Although the host chief gave of his treasure, his kinsmen and clan were obligated to chip in, too, for the prestige accruing to the host was also showered on the lesser folk in proportion to their status in the community.

Exceptionally wealthy chiefs were known occasionally to have dashed valuable coppers to bits—a likely reason so few remain—as convincing proof of wealth and power. Such an action also put in their places boastful guests, who could not afford a similar demonstration.

By and large, however, the potlatch confirmed inherited and earned rights and represented a capital investment, since guests were obligated—throughout Totemland—to return the invitation and to provide gifts not only of equal value but with interest. Some Kwakiutl chiefs expected as much as double in return, but the average interest was probably more on the order of twenty percent.

In the upper Skeena River country near Kitwancool land are several picturesque Indian villages like this one on Highway No. 16 near Hazelton, British Columbia. (British Columbia Government)

The potlatch, showy as it was, actually was something of a public court with the economic advantage that it increased trade, developed skills, promoted pride, and did much to produce the highest aboriginal living standard in North America. Scarcely anyone went hungry.

Personal initiative and skill enabled any person—even a commoner—to give a potlatch when he had amassed the necessary wherewithal. The right to own private property—along with respect for clan and tribal boundaries—became almost second nature to most Indians, and children were trained effectively in the thrifty use of time and in traditional filial and spiritual devotion.

Today, in isolated areas, an occasional native potlatch of sorts is celebrated but without great fanfare, and one can view a few remaining totem poles, still respected and owned with pride, in out-of-the-way places. Long may they stand in salute to the vigorous Pacific Northwest Coast Indian nations. Their gatherings are no more, but we may reasonably compare them with the great diplomatic affairs in our nation's capital where the ceremonies are equally dramatic and equally misunderstood.

10

Where to See Totem Poles Today

The aboriginal mysticism of North American Indians has always confounded those whose personal philosophy demands, or pretends to demand, a final and unchangeable answer to every mystery in the universe. Consequently, there have been too few persons in influential positions to sponsor the proper preservation of more than a minute fraction of the artifacts of Totemland. Where mysticism, and an intuitive oneness with nature, produced a colorful and descriptive substitute for a regional babel of tongues lacking written languages, totem poles filled the native requirements; they deserve preservation.

European civilization, by land and by sea, had smothered the native culture by 1890. A few anthropologists and historians were belatedly struck with the necessity to preserve, in the interests of future generations, some examples of the aboriginal arts. Several sought to interest the governments of the United States and Canada, but until recent years they were met with comparative coolness. The quest of each nation was for the most rapid possible colonization and commercialization of the Northwest Coast; few cared to preserve anything of the past regardless of the lessons to be learned.

If any one person was largely responsible for systematically promoting a program of preservation of totem poles, it was James Deans, who prevailed upon the 1893 Chicago World's Fair management to recognize this unique art and, himself, laboriously collected about a dozen Haida poles for that fair.

As the twentieth century boomed, Dr. C. F. Newcombe and his son W. A. Newcombe, Marius Barbeau of the National Museum of Canada, Franz Boas, and Wilson Duff of the British Columbia Provincial Museum were primarily instrumental in enlisting the support of various cultural institutions in the United

Totemic or heraldic screens, such as secluded the chief's apartment in the great houses, are rare today. This Tlingit screen in the Alaska State Museum in Juneau is a favorite with visitors like these Chee-chakoes when they visit the forty-ninth state. In "the old days" the screens were rough-hewn. (Pacific Northern Airlines)

States, Canada, and Europe in gathering, restoring, and exhibiting totem poles and related artifacts.

With a few exceptions, the Indians had, by the third decade of this century, largely lost sight of their heritage. Since about 1930, by agreements with many scattered tribes, clans, and families, there has been a concentrated, though widely scattered, professional effort to preserve outstanding totem specimens. Here is a list of some of the museums at which some of the best of these artifacts of a vigorous and exciting people may be seen:

In the United States:
Alaska State Historical Museum, Juneau
American Museum of Natural History, New York City
Colorado Museum of Natural History, Denver
Cranbrook Institute of Science, Bloomfield Hills, Michigan
Denver Art Museum, Denver
Detroit Institute of Arts, Detroit
Field Museum of Natural History, Chicago
Los Angeles County Museum, Los Angeles
Lowie Museum of Anthropology, University of California, Berkeley
Museum of the American Indian, Heye Foundation, New York City
Museum of the University of Washington, Seattle
Museum of the University of Pennsylvania, Philadelphia
Old Fort Kearney Museum, Fort Kearney (U.S. 30), Nebraska
Peabody Museum, Harvard University, Cambridge
Portland Art Museum, Portland, Oregon
Southeast Museum of the North American Indian, Marathon, Florida
Skagway Trail of '98 Museum, Skagway, Alaska

In Canada
National Museum of Canada, Ottawa
British Columbia Provincial Museum, Victoria
University of British Columbia Museum, Vancouver
Jardin Zoologique, Quebec City, Quebec
McGill University Museum, Montreal
Royal Ontario Museum, Toronto

Skeena Treasure House (Indian-owned), Hazelton, British Columbia

In Europe
British Museum, London, England
Fox Warren Museum, Fox Warren, England
Pitt-Rivers Museum, Oxford, England
Royal Edinburgh Museum, Edinburgh, Scotland
Ethnological Museum, Stockholm, Sweden
Museum für Völkerkunde, Berlin, Germany
Musée de l'Homme, Paris, France

Happily in recent years there has been an awakening of interest in the historical past on the part of Indians and whites alike along the Pacific Northwest Coast. Particularly has this been evident in British Columbia and Alaska, where land has wisely been set aside for development as public parks with emphasis on native architecture, restored poles, and authentic duplications of totem poles that have decayed with age.

Americans and Canadians are travelers by nature, and there are several vacation routes that meander through the traditional homelands of the totem-pole-carving Indians.

One of nature's loveliest regions is the Olympic Peninsula in Washington and the adjacent Puget Sound country. U.S. Highway 101 loops around the peninsula, where sharp eyes can still spot a few old but preserved remnants of totem poles at such places as Lake Quinault and nearby Amanda Park, Queets, Bogachiel, and in La Push, where a few members of the small and distinctive Quilliute nation still reside in their own village near a marvelous ocean-fishing harbor.

At Forks one can turn northward to U.S. 9A which skirts the Straits of Juan de Fuca. Driving west, one soon comes to the reservation of the Makah, the only Nootka tribe to establish itself in what is now American territory. A good gravel road leads from the little city of Neah Bay through the lush rain-forest tunnels to within a mile or so of historic Cape Flattery. Offshore is Tatooch Island, a wind-swept lighthouse station named for a historic Makah

These little Indians in remote regions deep in Tsimsyan country are still rather curious when tourists drive through their villages where a few old totem poles can still be seen. Though weathered and without paint, the totem figures are still in good condition. (British Columbia Government)

Totemland offers some of the hemisphere's finest river fishing, and its Indians, who are expert fishermen, still rely heavily on salmon as a staple for the dinner table. This is real white water, common on the Northwest Coast. (British Columbia Government)

This fine stand of old preserved poles is now in a public park at Klawock on Prince of Wales Island in Alaska, once shared by the southern Tlingit and Kaigani-Haida. Alaska and British Columbia have the finest collections of genuine totem poles. (Alaska Travel Division)

chief. This island was the scene of old-time Nootka whaling operations and—incredible as it may seem—was the landfall of at least one Japanese junk crew that drifted by currents from the Empire of the Rising Sun two hundred or more years ago. This event is said to have been responsible for introducing iron cutting tools to the Makah and adjacent Quil-

liute and Salish tribes. This, frankly, is open to conjecture, for the Spanish had explored most of the shores in this vicinity prior to that time. Tourist facilities, both modern and rustic, abound; the fishing and hunting are superb; and the enterprising Quinault Indians offer dugout canoe trips down "their river."

Port Angeles is a practical port from which

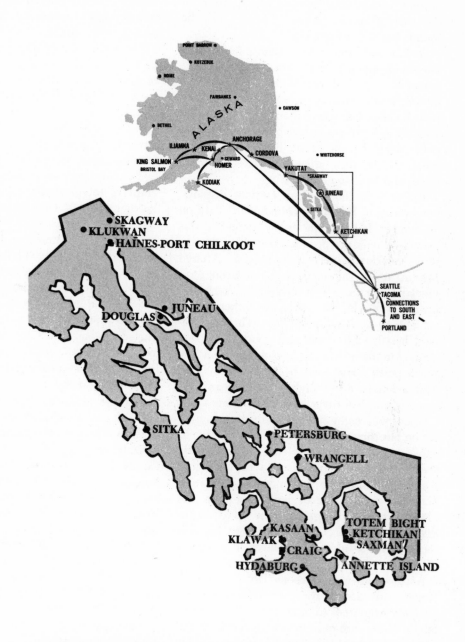

The principal areas in southeastern Alaska where restored totem poles can be viewed are shown on this area map. (Pacific Northern Airlines)

to embark by auto ferry to Victoria. Sequim (pronounced *skwim*) and Port Townsend also offer unusual sights; the latter's prime attraction is the century-old labyrinth of underground tunnels and the tong headquarters of the early Chinese. Indian artifacts can be found upon inquiring locally.

On the mainland, a few totem poles can be seen in Olympia, Tacoma, Seattle, and Everett where U.S. 99 leads across the most peaceful international boundary on earth to Vancouver, British Columbia, where Stanley Park displays scientifically preserved totem poles in an outdoor setting. Up the Fraser River valley a few poles can be seen around towns like Ruby Creek and Harrison Hot Springs.

Probably the finest of all outdoor displays, however, is in Victoria's Thunderbird Park on Vancouver Island. The many poles in this provincial park are presided over by a hereditary Kwakiutl chief, Nakapenkim (Mungo Martin), under the aegis of the adjacent Provincial Museum, which houses the finest collection of masks, weapons, and other native artifacts to be found anywhere. This huge island has fine highways and good side roads leading to towns where one can still see a few totem poles surrounded by green forests; accommodations are abundant at Duncan, Nanaimo, Campbell River, and similar places.

Those who enjoy traveling in sight of civilization but through near virgin country should drive north to Prince George via Canada roads 7, 12, and 97 and thence west through a wonderland of forests, mountains, and lakes to Hazelton in Kitwancool land. There in the Skeena Treasure House, modern Tsimsyan Indians display artifacts of their own nation plus those of the Kwakiutl and Haida in a replica of an old-time native community house.

A drive down the Skeena River to Prince Rupert is rewarding, for one travels where the ancients migrated to and from the ocean's edge. Here, around Prince Rupert, many tribes and clans of the Kwakiutl gathered a bit less than a hundred years ago in a loose confederation. Here was the last stand of their once-mighty culture. Here were held the final

frantic but wasteful potlatches where great wealth was given away, sometimes destroyed, in a gasping effort to sustain a tradition being choked to death by the white man's zeal to "civilize," which forced the native into a new and strange conformity that destroyed his oneness with nature.

The totem spirits also await the interested visitor to Alaska's panhandle, where the state of Alaska, the United States Federal Government, and most of the local people and communities have cooperated to establish totem parks in and near several towns. One travels either by ship or airplane in this maritime land of the Kaigani-Haida and Tlingit. Indeed one exclusively regional airline, Pacific Northern, employs totem symbols as an interior-decorating motif and, with connecting local charter services and feeder lines, enables the traveler seeking Indian atmosphere to be comfortably transported to places at which Indian artifacts and seasonal ceremonial events can be seen.

Some industries are beginning to take an interest in the ancient totem crafts. The Standard Oil Company of California recently employed Chilkat and Chilkoot carvers to make an authentic pole for the entrance to Alaska's first oil refinery near Kenai. Such encouragement is long overdue.

But the potlatch——you are not likely to hear of one, much less see one. Occasionally a descendant of the Raven, the Eagle, the Grizzly, or Frog will observe that he and his family are "Christians now and we are not supposed to erect totem poles." If rapport is established, he may go on to say, "But this does not make sense because the Bible does not say it is wrong to have totem poles."

What can one say? The Indian is correct; his poles were *not* gods to him, neither were they images to be worshiped. They were merely his billboard. But the potlatch, nevertheless, is discouraged.

The native art of the Northwest Pacific Coast was an integral part and manifestation of the infinite order that provided a beneficent environment. This order—nature or the "inner spirit" power of all creatures in the universe—

Visitors to Totem Bight near Ketchikan, Alaska, can stoop and enter the restored native Tlingit community house. The full width painting portrays Raven. The house-front pole figures shown are Raven (with beak) and Raven's mother, in human form, wearing a large labret in her lower lip. (Pacific Northern Airlines)

Leggings, masks, dancing aprons, pyramidal hats, and headdresses worn by these Tlingit dancers of the Chilkat tribe are authentic, as are their traditional annual performances at Haines-Port Chilkoot in Alaska. (Alaska Travel Division)

Displaying a typically stylized symbolization of a sea monster, this Kwakiutl house-front structure and the painting on it were made especially for Thunderbird Park in Victoria, British Columbia. The Kwakiutl memorial pole shows (from top down) Thunderbird, Wolf, a man, Beaver, and the female Cannibal Giant Dsonqua holding her child.

provided the impetus for the regionally unique aboriginal arts that were never practiced merely to occupy space. Rather than creating art for art's sake, the Indians of Totemland sought to show—usually by symbolization—the vitality and drama of life. If their art seems "distorted" or violent, it is because the viewer gazes either with relative complacency or little understanding, whereas the Indian, "in the old days," saw all creatures in a different perspective. In tune with nature, the Indian sought only to enjoy it as it was—and nature, like their art, is often violent.

Can we understand the ancient arts of Totemland? Can we "read" the poles? Yes and no, respectively, but, with a knowledge of the ancient traditional stories, they can be clearly interpreted. This is why I have written this book, a respectful and admiring effort to throw light on a vanishing culture in which the individual could seek and attain both spiritual and temporal identity.

Kla-ha-ya!

Appendix

"Nations" and Subdivisions of Totemland People

TLINGIT

Phratries: Raven (Yehl) and Wolf (Goch) or Eagle (Chak).

Tribes: (geographical groups principally)
Auk, Chilkat, Henya, Huna, Hutsnuwu, Kake, Kuiu, Sanyakoan, Sitka, Stikine, Sumdum, Tagish, Taku, Tongas, Yakutat (Hlahayik), Gunaho, Guthleuh.

HAIDA

Moieties: Raven (Hoya) and Eagle (Got); each divided into many clans.

Divisions: Haida proper (Gao-Haidagai): Graham and Moresby Islands.
Gunghet (or Kunghit): Kunghit and Anthony Islands.
Kaigani (Kets-hade): Prince of Wales and Long Islands.

Tribes: Not generally considered in the social structure as most groups took the name of their town to identify themselves.

TSIMSYAN (*or Chimmesyan*)

Phratries: Eagle, Grizzly Bear, Raven, Wolf; each phratry was further divided into numerous clans including Salmon-Eater, Bear, Flicker, Beaver, Dogfish, Frog, Killer Whale, etc.

Divisions and Tribes:
Tsimsyan proper tribes: Kilutsai, Kinagingee, Kinuhtoiah, Kishpachlaots, Kitkatla, Kitkahta, Kitlani, Kitsalthlal, Kitunto, Kilwilgioks (chief outranked all others), Kitwailksheba, Kitzeesh, Kitzilas, Kitzimgaylum, Kittizoo, Wudstae.
Niskae tribes: Kitkahteen, Kitlakdamix, Kitwinshilk, and Kitanweliks.
Gitksan tribes: Kauldaw, Kishgagass, Kishpiyeoux (Kispiox is present town name), Kitanmaiksh, Kitwingach, Kitwinskole (or Kitwancool), and Kitzegulka.

BELLA COOLA (sometimes called "Talion nation")

Tribes: Kinisquit, Noothlakimish, and Nuhalk.

KWAKIUTL

Divisions and Tribes:
Kwakiutl proper: Klaskino, Koprino, Koskimo, Quatsino, Nakomgilisala, Tlatasikoala, Await-

lala, Goasila, Guauaenok, Hahuamis, Hoya-
las, Keoksotenok, Kwakiutl, Matilpe, Lekwil-
tok, Mamalelekala, Nakoaktok, Nimkish,
Tenaktak, Tlauitsis, and Tsawatenok.

Haisla tribes: Kitamat, Kitlope, and Xaixais.

Heiltsuk tribes: Bellabella and China Hat.

NOOTKA

Tribes: Asousaht, Chaicclesaht, Clayoquot, Coop-
tee, Ehatisaht, Ekoolthaht, Hachaath, Hesquiat,
Kelsemaht, Klahosaht, Kwoneatshatka, Kyuquot, Makah, Manosaht, Mooachaht, Muchalat,
Nitinat, Nuchatlitz, Oiaht, Opitchesaht, Pa-
cheenaht, Seshart, Toquart, Uchucklesit, and
Uchielet.

COAST SALISH

Divisions and Tribes:

Comox: Comox proper, Homalko, Kaake, Ka-
kekt, Seechelt, Sliammon, Tatpoos, Hwah-
watl, Puntlatsh, and Saamen.

Cowichan: Clemclemalats, Comiakin, Hellelt,
Kenipsim, Kilpanlus, Koksilah, Kulleets, Lil-
malche, Malakut, Nanaimo, Penelakut, Qua-
michan, Siccameen, Snonowas, Somenos,
Tateke, Yekolaos, Chehalis, Chilliwack, Co-
quitlam, Ewawoos, Katzie, Kelatl, Kwantlem,
Matsqui, Musqueam, Nehaltmoken, Nico-
men, Ohamil, Pilalt, Popkum, Samahquam,
Scowlitz, Sewathen, Siyita, Skwawalooks,
Snonkweametl, Squawtits, Sumass, Tsakuam.

Squamish: Squamish proper, and Nooksak.

Songish: Clallam, Lummi, Samish, Sanetch,
Semiahmoo, Songish proper, and Sooke.

Nisqually: Duwamish, Nisqually proper, Puyallup, Skagit, Snoquamish, Squaxon, Etak-
mehu, Kwehtlmamish, Nukwatsamish, Nu-
sehtasatle, Potoashees, Sahewamish, Saku-
mehu, Samamish, Sawamish, Sekamish, Sho-
mamish, Shotlemamish, Skihwamish, Skopa-
mish, Smulkamish, Squacum, Stehtsasamish,
Steilacoomamish, Suquamish, and Towahhah.

Twana: Twana proper and Sailuspun.

Chehalis: Quinault, Quaitso, Humptulips, Chehalis, and Satsop.

QUILLIUTE:

Tribes: Quilliute proper, and Hoh.

Northwest Coast Mythology

Index